SHADOW & LIGHT: A Guide to Healing the Hidden Self

Copyright ® 2025 by Dr. Constance Santego.

Copy Editor and Interior Design: Constance Santego
Book Layout: ®2017 BookDesignTemplates.com

Ordering Information:
Quantity sales. Special discounts are available on quantity purchases by corporations, associations, and others. For details, contact the address below.

Trade paperback ISBN: 978-1-997907-14-5
eBook ISBN 978-1-997907-15-2

Created and published In Canada. Printed and bound in the United States of America

First Edition
Published by Maximillian Enterprises
Kelowna, BC Canada
www.constancesantego.ca

SHADOW & LIGHT: A Guide to Healing the Hidden Self

Dr. Constance Santego

Maximillian Enterprises
Kelowna, BC

Dedication

To every survivor who thought their shadow was a weakness.

It was your shield,
your compass,
your initiation.

You are the light you have been searching for.

"The shadow is not where we are broken. It is where we hid the parts of ourselves that needed to survive."

ALSO BY DR. CONSTANCE SANTEGO

NOVELS
Illegitimate Grace
Ashcroft Hollow

Okanagan Trilogy:
Beneath the Vineyards
Under the Okanagan Sun
Guardian of the Lake

The Nine Spiritual Gifts Series:
Journey of a Soul – (Vol 1 Michael)
Language of a Soul – (Vol 2 Gabriel)
Prophecy of a Soul – (Vol 3 Bath Kol)
Healing of a Soul – (Vol 4 Raphael)
Miracles of a Soul – (Vol 5 Hamied)
Knowledge of a Soul – (Vol 6 Raziel)
Wisdom of a Soul – (Vol 7 Uriel)
Faith of a Soul – (Vol 8 Pistis Sophia)

NONFICTION
The Intuitive Life, The Gift Of Prophecy, Third Edition
Fairy Tales, Dreams And Reality… *Where Are You On Your Path? Second Edition*
Your Persona… The Mask You Wear
Archangel Michael's Soul Retrieval Guide
Bend, Don't Break: *Finding Your Way Back To Abundance*
Ring Therapy: *A Guide To Healing And Balance*
Ring Therapy Pocket Guide
Beyond The Mind: *Harnessing The Power Of Astral Projection For Creative Awakening*
Floraopathy˚: *The Art And Science Of Vibrational Healing With Essential Oils*
Dear Older Me: A Memoir… *Of Sorts*
It's Just Like Poker: *A Spiritual Guide To Playing The Cards Life Deals You*
Signs And Meanings: *What The Feet Reveal About Health, Stress, And The Body's Story*
Auricions: *Unlocking Subconscious Healing Through Quantum Medicine*

Quick Fix Acupressure Method
Manifestation – *The DREAM Method In 5 Steps*
Confidence – *Mastering the Dream Method*
The New Paradigm: *Conscious Healing In The Age Of Ai*

TESLA SERIES:
Tesla And The Future Of Energy Medicine
Beyond Tesla: *Advancing The Science Of Energy Healing*
Tesla's Code: *Mastering Energy, Frequency, And Creative Power*
Tesla's Bioenergetic Blueprint: *Healing the Human Field Through Frequency, Mapping & Coherence*

SECRETS OF A HEALER, SERIES:
Magic Of Aromatherapy (Vol I)
Magic Of Reflexology (Vol II)
Magic Of The Gifts (Vol III)
Magic Of Muscle Testing (Vol IV)
Magic Of Iridology (Vol V)
Magic Of Massage (Vol VI)
Magic Of Hypnotherapy (Vol VII)
Magic Of Reiki (Vol VIII)
Magic Of Advanced Aromatherapy (Vol IX)
Magic Of Esthetics (Vol X)
The Reiki Master's Manual (Vol XI)

REIKI WISDOM, SERIES:
Angelic Lifestyle, a Vibrant Lifestyle
Angelic Lifestyle 42-Day Energy Cleanse
Reiki and the Power of The Joint Points: Unlocking Energy Pathways for Healing (Vol I)
Reiki and Karmic Healing: Releasing Patterns From Past Lives (Vol II)
Reiki and the Five Elements (Vol III)
Secrets of a Healer, Magic Of Reiki
The Reiki Master's Manual *(In English, German, Spanish, French, Portuguese, Russian, Hindi, and Mandarin Chinese)*
Reiki and Shadow Work: *Healing the Dark Side of the Soul*

CHAKRA SERIES:
Heart Chakra 101: The Bridge
Root Chakra 101: Building Safety, Survival, Foundation
Sacral Chakra 101: Creativity, Pleasure, Emotions
Solar Plexus Chakra 101: Power, Confidence, Will
Throat Chakra 101: Truth, Voice, Self-Expression
Third Eye Chakra 101: Intuition, Vision, Insight
Crown Chakra 101: Spiritual Connection, Transcendence.

ADULT COLORING JOURNALS
SERIES-ZEN COLORING:
Quantum Energy and Mindful Living Journal (Vol 1)
Reiki Energy Journal (Vol 2)
Nine Spiritual Gifts Journal (Vol 3)
I Forgive Journal (Vol 4)

FOR CHILDREN
I am Big Tonight. I Don't Need the Light
The Magic Elf Book: 25 Days of Surprises

COOKBOOK
My Favorite Recipes, with a Hint of Giggle

BUISNESS
How To Use ChatGPT For Authors: From Idea To Published Book
Scaling Beyond 6 Figures: Strategies For Health & Wellness Professionals
The Academypreneur's Playbook: Turn Knowledge Into A
Revenue-Generating School

HUMOR/GIFT BOOK
How Do You Like Your Eggs? *Crack Into Your Personality, Yolk and All*

Contents

Preface

A Light Held in the Dark

There are parts of our story that grow quiet over time.
Not because they are truly gone,
but because the body learned to carry them in silence.

Some memories blur.
Some feelings go numb.
Some truths hide beneath survival instincts so intelligent
that the child we once were managed to stay whole
even when the world around them was not.

This book was written for those quiet places.

It is not a record of darkness,
nor an excavation of pain.
It is an invitation into the inner space
where shadow and light meet —
where the forgotten, silenced, or misunderstood parts of us
have waited for someone to finally listen with compassion.

For many of us, shadow began in childhood,
in rooms where emotions were not safe,
or where truth was too heavy for young shoulders.
Fear, confusion, silence, caretaking, invisibility —
these were not flaws

but brilliant adaptations in an environment that required
sensitivity, stillness, or vigilance.

The shadow is not who you are.
It is who you became
to stay safe long enough to grow.

And now, you have grown.

This work does not chase memory,
force emotion,
or assign blame.
It simply asks that you hold space
for what once held space for you.

You will meet archetypes rooted in instinct.
You will see how the body remembers
even when the mind cannot.
You will trace the shape of beliefs formed long before
language,
and learn how to release the ones that are no longer needed.

Alongside reflection, you will find tools —
gentle, grounded, and born from years of working with
energy, intuition, and trauma-informed care:

- breathwork that signals safety
- Reiki sequences designed for emotional unwinding
- grounding practices
- and guided reparenting that allows the inner child to
  finally rest.

Healing the shadow does not erase the past.
It transforms our relationship to it.

You may discover that what once felt heavy
becomes a source of empathy, intuition, and spiritual depth.
You may find that emotional patterns make sense in a way
they never have before.
You may feel your voice soften, strengthen, or return.

And perhaps most importantly,
you may finally look at the child you once were
and see not a wound
but a miracle of wisdom and resilience.

This book is not a promise of instant healing.
It is a path of remembering
and a practice of meeting yourself with tenderness.

Take your time.
Pause when you need to.
Breathe deeply.
And let every page remind you
that you are worthy of slowness, gentleness, and compassion.

Your shadow does not define you.
It guided you.
It protected you.
It preserved pieces of you that you are now ready to reclaim.

May this work bring you back to the truth beneath every scar
—
that you survived,

you adapted,
and you are allowed to become whole.

Welcome to the light beyond the shadow.

Note to Reader

Note to the Reader

Before you begin, I want to offer you something important:

You do not need to force anything here.

Shadow work can be tender, surprising, and deeply personal.
It may stir memories, emotions, or physical sensations.
It may also bring silence, numbness, or nothing at all.
All of these responses are valid.

This book is a companion, not a command.
It is an invitation, not an excavation.
You are always in charge of the pace.

If any page feels too heavy, pause.
If a memory feels unclear, let it remain soft.
If emotions rise, breathe and return to grounding practices.
You do not need to push through discomfort to heal.

Shadow healing is not about reliving the past.
It is about understanding it with compassion
and meeting the child you once were
with gentleness instead of judgment.

You are encouraged to:

- notice your body
- listen to your breath

- pay attention to internal signals
- respect boundaries, even with yourself

Your nervous system holds incredible wisdom.
Trust it.
It will always tell you when to continue and when to rest.

And if, at any point, the material in this book awakens distress,
please consider reaching out to a trauma-informed therapist,
counselor, or support professional.
There is strength in receiving support,
and there is no shame in needing it.
Some journeys are easier with someone who can walk beside
you.

You deserve care, safety, and tenderness — not pressure.

Finally, remember this:
What rises to the surface here does not define you.
It reveals something about how you survived — how brilliantly
you adapted in circumstances that asked too much of you.

The deeper purpose of this work is not to reopen wounds,
but to relieve the parts of you that carried them alone.

So move slowly.
Meet each page with curiosity and compassion.
Honor the wisdom of your timing.

You are already healing simply by being willing to look inward
with kindness.

You are safe.
You are capable.
You are worthy.
And you are not alone.

Learning Outcome

What you will gain from this journey

By the end of this book, you will not be "finished" with your healing —
but you will have the awareness, tools, and inner clarity
to continue the journey with strength and compassion.

Here is what this work will help you cultivate:

1. A Deeper Understanding of Your Shadow

- Recognize how unconscious coping patterns were formed
- See your shadow as protection, not flaw
- Understand the difference between who you are and what you learned

2. Clarity About Your Childhood Emotional Environment

- Identify unspoken emotional rules
- Understand how atmosphere, power dynamics, and silence shaped the nervous system
- Recognize inherited fears versus lived experience

3. Recognition of Your Shadow Archetype(s)

- The Silent Child
- The Watcher
- The Protector

- The Disappearing Self
  Learn how each instinct was born from wisdom, sensitivity, and self-preservation.

4. Compassion for the Inner Child

- Witness childhood experiences with tenderness rather than judgment
- Understand why memories may be incomplete, blurred, or hidden
- Create emotional safety inside your adult self

5. Body-Based Awareness of Stored Memory

- Identify where tension, fear, or silence sit in the body
- Understand freeze, fawn, fight, and flight responses
- Learn how nervous-system imprinting occurs

6. Shadow Healing Practices for Integration

- Reiki-based hand placements for emotional release
- Breathwork designed to signal safety
- Grounding rituals, aura cleansing, and energetic realignment
- Techniques for dissolving old survival beliefs at the root

7. Tools for Rewriting Childhood Beliefs

- Identify the core belief formed in early years
- Understand how that belief shaped behaviour, identity, relationships, and spirituality
- Replace survival patterns with aligned truths

8. Self-Protection that is Healthy, Not Reactive

- Build boundaries without guilt
- Speak your truth without fear
- Hold emotional sovereignty without collapsing or disappearing

9. Recognition of the Gifts Born from Shadow

- Intuition
- Empathy
- Discernment
- Spiritual depth
- Emotional intelligence
- Leadership and compassion
  Learn how to keep these gifts while releasing the fear that created them.

10. Signs of Healing and Integration

- Awareness of internal shifts
- Emotional softness around past memories
- Greater presence in the body
- Authentic voice returning
- The ability to meet yourself with kindness

11. A New Relationship With Your Past

Not rewritten,
not erased — but held with truth, peace, and clarity.

You will discover that the past no longer defines you.
It informs you, strengthens you, and eventually transforms into wisdom.

What is not expected of you

This book does **not** ask you to:

- relive pain
- force memories
- rush healing
- confront more than you are ready for

There is no finish line.

Shadow healing is the lifelong practice
of meeting yourself honestly and gently.

The Heart of These Outcomes

By the final page, my hope is that you will feel:

- safer inside your own body
- more compassionate toward your younger self
- less defined by what you survived
- and more connected to the person you are becoming

You will know how to sit with yourself,
how to listen inwardly,
and how to approach shadow with understanding rather than
fear.

And ultimately —
how to stand in your own light
without hiding any part of who you are.

Introduction

A journey into the shadows that shaped you — and the light you were born to reclaim.

Everyone carries a shadow.

Not because we are broken.
Not because we are weak.
But because, at some point in our lives, we had to hide parts of ourselves to survive.

We learned to stay quiet when we wanted to speak.
We learned to be strong when we wanted to cry.
We learned to sense danger before anyone else noticed it.
We learned to shrink, to disappear, or to become the caretaker long before we understood what those roles meant.

The shadow is not the darkness inside us.
It is the part of us that once protected us.

And at some point in adulthood, we begin to feel the weight of what we once hid:

- the fear we absorbed but never understood,
- the silence we kept because it felt safer than truth,
- the confusion of childhood moments we still can't fully place,
- the emotional imprints we inherited from the people around us,
- and the lingering sense that something inside us is still waiting to be seen.

This book is an invitation to that hidden place.

It is not a book of therapy, nor is it a retelling of trauma.
Instead, it is a gentle companion for those who feel:

- something in their past shaped them deeply,
- something in their body still remembers what the mind cannot,
- something in their life patterns keeps repeating,
- and something within them is ready—finally—to heal.

You do not need to remember every detail of your childhood to heal your shadow.
You do not need to relive anything painful.
You do not need to "fix" yourself.

What you need is clarity, compassion, and a safe way to meet the parts of yourself that were pushed into the dark.

In these pages, you will explore:

- how shadows form,
- how children absorb fear and silence,
- how intuition is born through survival,
- how the body holds memories the mind protects us from,
- and how you can dissolve old patterns with tenderness instead of force.

You will also walk beside me through parts of my own journey—told safely, simply, and honestly—not to relive the past, but to illuminate the path forward. My story is not included to shock or burden, but to say:

"You are not alone.
You are not imagining it.
And you are not broken."

The heart of this book is the return to yourself.
The parts you hid.
The strength you didn't know you had.
The light that was never extinguished—only waiting for the right moment to be reclaimed.

This is that moment.

May this book be a sanctuary for your healing,
a mirror for your truth,
and a reminder that even the deepest shadows point toward the brightest light.

You were born for more than survival.
You were born to reclaim yourself fully.

Let us begin.

Dr. Constance Santego
Grand Reiki Master

SECTION I — THE NATURE OF THE SHADOW

CHAPTER 1 — What The Shadow Really Is

The shadow is not the darkness within you — it is the part of you that once kept you safe.

Most people think their "shadow" is the part of themselves they don't like:

- the anger they hide,
- the fear they silence,
- the insecurities they bury,
- the reactions they don't understand,
- the parts of themselves they judge harshly.

But the truth is far more compassionate.

The shadow is not your flaw.
The shadow is your **protection**.

The shadow is the part of you that stepped forward when you were small and didn't have words for what you felt.
It was born the moment you learned to adapt in order to survive.

The shadow is the child who:

- stayed quiet so no one would get angry,
- became invisible so no one would get hurt,
- watched everything because unpredictability felt dangerous,

- took care of others to keep the peace,
- or held in emotions because there was no safe place to let them out.

This is the real shadow.

Not darkness.
Not brokenness.
Not shame.

But a **younger part of you** that learned how to survive the world you were born into.

THE SHADOW IS NOT THE ENEMY

It is misunderstood, yes.
But not harmful.

The shadow kept you:

- safe,
- small when you needed to be,
- quiet when speaking wasn't an option,
- alert when danger was near,
- and protected when the world around you felt too big, too loud, or too unpredictable.

Your shadow is the part of you that said:

"I'll carry this for now, so you can get through this."

And it did.
For years.

WHY THE SHADOW SHOWS UP IN ADULTHOOD

By the time we reach adulthood, the world we live in is no longer the world we grew up in.

But the body doesn't know that.

The shadow carries *old rules*, such as:

- "Don't speak up; it's not safe."
- "Stay small; attention brings danger."
- "People can't be trusted."
- "If you make a mistake, something bad will happen."
- "I must take care of others first."
- "I must stay alert; safety depends on me."

Your adult self might look calm, successful, insightful, and wise…

And yet your shadow-self may still be holding childhood beliefs:

- the belief that the world is unsafe,
- the belief that you will be punished for being yourself,
- the belief that emotions are dangerous,
- the belief that you are responsible for others' feelings,
- or the belief that your needs don't matter.

This mismatch — between the adult reality and the child-formed shadow — is what creates:

- anxiety,
- overthinking,
- shutting down,
- people-pleasing,
- perfectionism,
- emotional triggers,

- self-sabotage,
- difficulty trusting,
- fear of conflict,
- or feeling "stuck."

Not because something is wrong with you.

But because your shadow hasn't realized you're safe now.

SHADOW WORK ISN'T ABOUT DIGGING THROUGH PAIN

This is where many people misunderstand shadow work.

Shadow work isn't:

- reliving old trauma
- forcing yourself to remember
- confronting people
- diving into darkness
- breaking yourself open

Shadow work is:

- compassion
- understanding
- recognition
- integration
- letting go of fear
- welcoming back a part of yourself that has been alone too long

The shadow is healed through gentleness, not force.

Through awareness, not intensity.

Through **presence**, not pressure.

Through **self-compassion**, not self-judgment.

THE SHADOW IS BORN FROM INCOMPLETE CHILDHOOD EXPERIENCES

A child sees the world differently than an adult does.

If a child experiences:

- yelling,
- fear,
- unpredictability,
- silence,
- confusion,
- instability,
- or witnessing others' distress,

the child interprets it emotionally, not logically.

They don't think:

"**Mom is under stress.**"
They think:
"**I must be the problem.**"

They don't think:

"**Dad is unstable.**"
They think:
"**I need to stay quiet so nothing bad happens.**"

The shadow is created in those moments — not from what happened, but from what the child *understood* about what happened.

Those early interpretations become lifelong beliefs.

Shadow work gently rewrites them.

THE SHADOW IS NOT A THREAT — IT IS AN INVITATION

Your shadow shows up when you are ready for your next level of healing.

Not to scare you.
Not to overwhelm you.
Not to drag you backward.

The shadow arises when it trusts that your adult self is strong enough, aware enough, and grounded enough to meet it.

This book is a journey into that meeting.

Into the part of you that once carried fear so you could survive…
and the part of you now ready to carry light so you can thrive.

Because the shadow was never meant to be permanent.

It was only meant to protect you until you were strong enough to heal it.

And you are strong enough now.

THE JUNGIAN CONCEPT OF THE SHADOW

Carl Jung, the Swiss psychiatrist and mystic, described the shadow as:

"The part of the personality that the ego does not wish to see."

Not because it's evil.
Not because it's dangerous.
But because it carries:

- pain,
- fear,
- unmet needs,
- old memories,
- and truths we once felt unprepared to face.

Jung didn't see the shadow as darkness.

He saw it as the unintegrated self—the parts of us we hid so we could survive.

In Jung's view:

- The shadow always wants to be integrated.
- It rises not to harm us, but to be healed.
- It holds the keys to our authenticity.
- It contains our suppressed gifts as much as our suppressed pain.

This is why he said:

"The shadow is 90% pure gold."

And he was right.

EMOTIONAL SHADOWS — NOT "BADNESS"

The shadow does not contain evil qualities.
It contains emotional residues:

- the fear a child had when someone yelled,
- the shame a child took on when an adult was unstable,
- the silence a child learned to survive conflict,
- the vigilance a child used to stay safe,
- the guilt a child felt for things that were never their responsibility.

These become emotional shadows.

Not because you did anything wrong.
But because your younger self tried to make sense of a world that felt larger than they were.

Shadow work is not about "fixing" these emotions.
It is about meeting them, gently and compassionately, and letting them integrate into your adult self.

WHY WE FEAR OUR OWN HIDDEN PARTS

We fear the shadow for two reasons:

1. Because we once needed to hide it to survive

As children, we hide parts of ourselves because:

- expressing fear wasn't safe
- having needs wasn't allowed
- speaking up caused conflict
- being visible brought threat
- emotions were too big for the adults around us

What we hide for safety becomes the shadow.

2. Because the shadow holds truths we've avoided

Some truths feel overwhelming until we are older, such as:

- "I didn't feel safe."
- "I wasn't supported emotionally."
- "I absorbed the pain of others."
- "I learned to disappear."
- "I was carrying responsibility that wasn't mine."

But when the adult self finally has the capacity to face these truths…
the shadow rises not to scare us, but because it is safe to heal now.

THE SHADOW AS A PROTECTOR

The shadow formed to keep you alive.

It said:

- "Stay small so they won't yell."
- "Stay quiet so nothing bad happens."
- "Be good so you don't cause trouble."
- "Watch everything so you can prepare."
- "Don't cry—it's not safe to show emotion."
- "Disappear until the danger passes."

This was *not dysfunction.*
This was wisdom.

The shadow is a survival strategy from a time when you needed protection.

The problem arises when:

- the childhood situation ends
- but the survival strategies continue
- even though your adult life is now safe

This is why people feel stuck:

The shadow is still trying to protect you using old rules.

Shadow work updates the rules.

THE SHADOW AS AN INTELLIGENCE

The shadow is not primitive.
It is not irrational.
It is not useless.

It is a highly intelligent part of you that:

- remembers emotional patterns
- tracks danger
- senses people's motives
- retains childhood intuition
- keeps deep memories
- knows what hurt and why
- tries to warn you before repeating old pain

In spiritual terms:

The shadow is the intuition of the wounded child.
The higher self is the intuition of the healed adult.
Shadow work unites the two.

When integrated, the shadow becomes:

- your strongest intuition
- your protective wisdom
- your emotional intelligence
- your empathy
- your resilience
- your spiritual depth
- your authenticity
- your courage

The shadow is not something to overcome.
It is something to welcome home.

IN SUMMARY: WHAT THE SHADOW REALLY IS

- It is the unhealed part of your past.
- It is the emotion you weren't allowed to feel.
- It is the truth you weren't allowed to speak.
- It is the fear you absorbed from others.
- It is the younger you who learned to survive.
- It is the protector who kept you safe.
- It is the intelligence waiting to be integrated.

It is not darkness.
It is the part of your light you were once forced to hide.

CHAPTER 2 — Childhood: The Birthplace of the Shadow

Children don't live inside facts; they live inside the emotional atmosphere that surrounds them.

Childhood is where our first shadows form — not because terrible things happened (although sometimes they did), but because our nervous system was still developing, and our emotional understanding of the world was fragile, instinctive, and unfiltered.

Adults remember events logically.

Children remember how it felt.

And when a child feels unsafe, confused, unseen, silenced, or responsible for the moods of others, the shadow begins to take shape.

This chapter is not about blaming childhood or parents.
It is about understanding the environment that shaped the unconscious parts of us, where fear still lingers.

Let's explore how and why this happens.

HOW CHILDREN ABSORB ATMOSPHERE

A child's developing mind is not analytical.
It is sensory.

Children feel:

- tone of voice,
- emotional pressure,
- tension in the air,
- facial expressions,
- unpredictable reactions,
- fear in adults,
- silence heavy with unspoken truths.

Even when a child cannot understand adult problems, they sense the emotional climate surrounding them.

For a child:

- anger feels like danger,
- silence feels like rejection,
- intensity feels like instability,
- emotional inconsistency feels like confusion.

The atmosphere becomes the child's instruction manual.

They learn:

- When to hide
- When to stay quiet
- When to anticipate danger
- When to take emotional responsibility
- When to become a peacekeeper

And most importantly:

They learn who they must become in order to stay physically and emotionally safe.

These learned roles become shadow patterns later in life.

WHY FEAR "STICKS" IN THE CHILDHOOD BODY

Children cannot rationalize fear.

To a child, fear is not a moment — it is a world.

The nervous system absorbs fear as a primal truth:

- "The world is unstable."
- "I must be careful."
- "Something bad could happen at any moment."
- "My safety depends on other people's moods."

When a child senses that safety is unpredictable, the body encodes that fear as survival programming.

And the body does this brilliantly.

It stores the memory even when the mind tries to protect us from remembering.

Fear sticks because the body believes:

"If I remember this feeling, I can protect myself in the future."

WHEN TRUTH BECOMES CONFUSED

Children do not understand adult emotions or adult causes.

So they assign meaning based on what they can feel.

A child sees:

- yelling = I'm in danger
- silence = I did something wrong
- tension = I should disappear
- sadness in adults = I am the problem
- inconsistency = I must be hyper-aware

This emotional logic becomes the foundation of the shadow.

The child is not interpreting reality.

They are interpreting atmosphere.

They don't know:

- a parent is under financial stress
- a family member is depressed
- an adult has unresolved trauma
- or that someone's instability has nothing to do with them

But the child's nervous system needs an explanation.

So it creates the only one it can:

"Something must be wrong with me."

The original truth is lost.

The emotional interpretation becomes the shadow.

THE DIFFERENCE BETWEEN TRAUMA AND FEAR-IMPRINTS

Not every shadow comes from trauma.

Many shadows come from moments that were:

- emotionally charged
- confusing
- unpredictable
- overwhelming
- silent
- unresolved
- misunderstood

Trauma is an event.

A fear-imprint is an emotional conclusion.

For example:

Trauma:
An adult screams aggressively at a child.

> Fear-Imprint:
> The child decides:
> "I must never express myself, or I will be hurt."

Trauma:
Repeated neglect or emotional abandonment.

> Fear-Imprint:
> "I don't matter."

"I shouldn't need anything."
"Love can disappear at any moment."

Trauma:
Witnessing violence, chaos, or instability.

Fear-Imprint:
"I must stay alert at all times."
"It's my job to keep the peace."
"I should not trust my safety to anyone else."

A shadow can form even when the child does not consciously remember the moment — because the body remembers the emotion.

Trauma is what happened.
The shadow is the conclusion the child formed about themselves because of it.

WHY THE BODY REMEMBERS WHAT THE MIND FORGETS

The mind's job is protection.

Especially in childhood, the mind shields us from thoughts that are too large or too painful to process.

So it does something extraordinary:

- It buries details
- Erases images
- Softens memories
- Blocks clarity
- Creates gaps

Meanwhile…

The body holds the imprint.

It stores:

- the sensation of fear,
- the tension in the stomach,
- the instinct to hold your breath,
- the impulse to be silent,
- the freezing response,
- the urge to stay small,
- the emotional memories the mind refused to keep.

This is why adults sometimes feel:

- suddenly anxious
- triggered by tone
- overwhelmed by someone's anger
- scared without reason
- or deeply emotional for no logical cause

The body remembers a feeling that once kept you safe.

The mind doesn't show images because it believes:

"You don't need them to heal.
You only need to understand what you felt."

This is the core of shadow work.

Not reliving events —
but decoding the emotions the body held onto, so the adult self
can finally release them.

THE GENTLE TRUTH

Children are not shaped primarily by what happened to them…

…but by what they felt while it happened.

And what they believed about themselves because of it.

This is why one sibling remembers chaos, another remembers silence, and another remembers nothing at all.

The shadow is as unique as the child who formed it.

But the purpose is universal:

To keep the child safe until the adult is strong enough to understand.

And that is where you are now.

CHAPTER 3 — The Inner Child: Keeper of the Shadow

We outgrow our childhood, but the emotions we carried often do not. They wait within us, asking to be seen.

The inner child is not a metaphor.
It is not something imagined or symbolic.

The inner child is a psychological and emotional imprint — the part of us that still carries our earliest interpretations of the world:

- who we needed to be to survive,
- what we believed was required to stay safe,
- what we learned about love, fear, and silence,
- and the behaviors that once protected us.

Long after our bodies grow, the inner child remains within the subconscious.

It does not act like an adult.
It acts like the age we were when fear first arrived.

This is why certain emotions within us feel much younger than we are.

When we learn how to meet the inner child instead of ignoring them, something powerful happens:

The shadow begins to soften.

THE SILENT OBSERVER

Before a child has words, they have awareness.

Long before they understand sentences, they understand tone, danger, tension, frustration, emotional distance, and unspoken truths.

Even at two, three, four years old, a child can sense:

- when someone is angry,
- when someone is unpredictable,
- when someone is ashamed,
- when someone is lying,
- when someone is hurting inside,
- when something is unsafe,
- when they need to disappear.

Children become silent observers because silence is safer than questions.

They learn to watch everything:

- facial expressions,
- body language,
- footsteps,
- breathing patterns,
- emotional shifts,

always preparing for what might come next.

This silent witnessing is not weakness.
It is survival intelligence.

Later in life, that same sensitivity often becomes empathy, intuition, or spiritual awareness.

But during childhood, it is the beginning of the shadow.

THE FROZEN CHILD

When a child's nervous system detects danger — emotional or physical — the instinct is not always to fight or run.

Often, it is to freeze.

Freezing is the body's way of saying:

- "Be still."
- "Don't make noise."
- "Don't be visible."
- "Don't trigger anything."
- "Wait until the danger passes."

This freeze response is the nervous system's ancient protective mechanism.

It teaches the child:

- how to disappear,
- how to stay small,
- how to numb feelings,
- how to go silent,
- how to detach emotionally,
- how to survive without being seen.

Later in life, the "frozen child" shows up when adults:

- go quiet during conflict,
- disconnect during emotional conversations,
- numb themselves when stressed,

- shut down when overwhelmed,
- become small when criticized,
- lose their voice around authority,
- hide their true feelings to stay safe.

It is not immaturity.
It is childhood training that was never unlearned.

WHY WE DON'T REMEMBER EVERYTHING

Many people blame themselves for not recalling childhood moments clearly.

But forgetting is a protective gift.

The mind stores only what it believes we can handle.

Remembering is not a requirement for healing.

In fact, the body remembers far more accurately than the mind does.

When something is too overwhelming, too confusing, or too emotionally complex for a child to contextualize, the brain takes over and blocks details.

It doesn't erase truth.
It shields us from what we lacked the capacity to process.

This is why adults sometimes know *something happened* without remembering exactly what.

Healing does not come from recovering memories.

Healing comes from understanding how those moments shaped our emotional responses.

And that is the work of the inner child.

NERVOUS-SYSTEM IMPRINTING

Every emotional experience in childhood is recorded through the nervous system.

If a child repeatedly experiences:

- unpredictability,
- fear,
- stress,
- silence,
- instability,
- emotional pressure,

their nervous system adapts to survive it.

The adaptation becomes a pattern.

These imprints later show up as:

- anxiety,
- hypervigilance,
- people-pleasing,
- emotional numbness,
- avoidance,
- perfectionism,
- over-responsibility,
- shutting down under stress.

Nothing is wrong with the adult.

The body is simply following childhood programming.

The nervous system does not update automatically.

It needs conscious retraining.

Shadow work — especially when paired with energy healing — becomes that retraining.

HOW THE INNER CHILD INFLUENCES ADULT BEHAVIOUR

Even when our logical mind knows better...
the inner child still whispers old rules.

This is why an adult who knows they are safe might still feel unsafe.

Why someone successful might still fear failure.

Why someone loved might feel unworthy.

Why someone smart might keep shrinking.

Why someone strong might freeze in conflict.

And why certain triggers feel "bigger than they should."

Because the inner child believes:

- "I must stay small."
- "I must not make mistakes."
- "I must not upset anyone."
- "I must stay quiet to survive."
- "I must take care of others before myself."

These beliefs were once lifesaving.

Now they are outdated.

Shadow work is the process of letting the inner child know:

"You survived.
I'm here now.
We are safe."

When the adult self steps forward with presence, compassion, and emotional maturity, something extraordinary happens:

The shadow dissolves.

The inner child begins to relax.

And the nervous system learns a new truth:

Safety is no longer conditional.
It is internal.

IN THE END...

The inner child is not a wounded fragment.
They are the guardian of emotional truth.

They hold:

- what hurt,
- what frightened you,
- who you needed to be,
- and what you have yet to heal.

They are not your weakness.
They are the doorway to wholeness.

And when we meet them, listen to them, and bring them back into the light, our entire emotional world changes.

Because the inner child is not seeking perfection.

They are seeking only this:

A safe, loving adult within you who finally says:

"You don't have to protect me anymore.
I will protect you now."

SECTION II — MY JOURNEY THROUGH SHADOW

CHAPTER 4 — Early Life in the Storm

Some children grow up learning the world through language.
Others learn it through silence, through tension, through the
quiet observations that shape the soul.

We don't choose the environment we're born into.
We arrive as clean light — open, trusting, and receptive — and
then we begin absorbing everything that surrounds us.

For some, childhood is structured, stable, predictable.

For others, it is full of movement, uncertainty, silence, and
lessons that arrive long before the child is old enough to
understand them.

This is where many shadows begin.

This chapter is not a retelling of what happened in my
childhood.
It is an exploration of how the emotional environment around us
becomes the foundation of our inner world.

YOUNG PARENTS

My parents were very young when I was born.
Just teenagers themselves — barely stepping into adulthood,
still figuring out who they were, still finding their own footing
in life.

They did not yet have the emotional language to communicate their fears, insecurities, frustrations, or dreams.
And so much went unspoken.

Young parents often carry pressure they cannot name.
They're trying to grow up while raising a child.
They're managing their own wounds while learning how to keep another human safe.

When a child is raised by parents who are still healing from their own past — or still overwhelmed by the present — the child naturally becomes sensitive to emotional shifts.

I learned very early that safety was not always predictable.

And like many children in similar circumstances, I began to sense what others felt long before I spoke about what I felt.

MOVING OFTEN

In my earliest memories, life did not stand still.
Homes changed, environments shifted, familiar walls came and went.

To a young child, frequent moving is not just a change of scenery — it is instability felt in the body.
It teaches adaptability, yes.
But it also teaches quietness.

When the world keeps changing around you, you learn to hold your inner world tightly and silently.

You don't form deep attachments.
You stay alert.
You assess rooms before relaxing.
You learn to adjust quickly, without complaint.

This kind of childhood trains the nervous system to become attentive, responsive, and cautious.

Adults may remember just a series of addresses.
The child remembers the emotional atmosphere of each place.

And how quickly comfort could disappear.

LEARNING TO STAY QUIET

Many children learn to speak.
Some learn to silence themselves.

Silence is not always about being shy.
It can be an emotional skill — a way of making peace with unpredictability.

When adults are overwhelmed, stressed, or carrying their own burdens, children instinctively learn:

- not to ask questions,
- not to upset anyone,
- not to express needs,
- and not to be a source of pressure.

I learned to stay quiet.
I learned to move carefully within emotional spaces.
I learned to read people before I ever read books.

Silence became the safest place to breathe.

What I didn't know then — but understand now — is that children who learn to be silent are often highly intuitive.
Their silence isn't emptiness.
It is observation.

FEELING WHAT OTHERS DIDN'T SAY

Children in unstable environments develop a kind of emotional radar.

It doesn't come from fear alone.
It comes from necessity.

I could feel tension before voices rose.
I could sense when someone was hurting, even if they smiled.
I noticed what adults tried to hide, even when they said "everything is fine."
I understood emotional temperature without a single sentence spoken.

Many sensitive children share this.

They learn to detect danger the way some animals sense storms.

They pick up on tone, posture, silence, pacing, and energy.
They feel the unspoken truths, the compressed emotions, the stories no one wants to acknowledge.

It can be overwhelming.
But it is also the beginning of empathy, sensitivity, and spiritual awareness.

Adults sometimes carry spiritual gifts developed in childhood simply because they had to listen to the emotional world more than the verbal one.

BECOMING THE INTUITIVE CHILD

Many people assume intuition arrives in adulthood.

But the truth is, intuition is often forged in childhood.

It is born from:

- emotional alertness,
- pattern recognition,
- quiet observation,
- sensitivity to others,
- and the need to understand what is not being said.

Children who grow up learning to sense danger often carry that same awareness into adulthood.
Those who learned to read the atmosphere become healers, mediators, energy workers, and protectors later in life.

They become the people who can walk into a room and feel:

- who is hurting,
- who is anxious,
- who feels lonely,
- who is defensive,
- who is carrying a secret,
- and who is in need of compassion.

This is one of the greatest paradoxes of shadow childhood:

The same environment that creates wounds also awakens gifts.

The shadow child often becomes:

- an intuitive adult
- a healer
- an empath
- a guide
- a teacher
- a soul who walks gently in the world
- someone who sees beneath the surface

Because to make sense of what scared us, we had to understand the emotional truth behind it.

And that search for truth becomes a lifelong trait.

It is not darkness at all.

It is sensitivity refined — the ability to see beyond masks, feel through silence, and detect what others may not notice.

Many who choose the path of healing later in life began by surviving childhood emotionally.

They didn't just get through it —
they learned how to listen to the world in a different language.

A language made of:

energy,
instinct,
knowing,
and empathy.

And for many of us, it becomes our deepest calling...
to help others feel the light that we had to cultivate in the dark.

CHAPTER 5 — Survival Through Stillness

Silence is not emptiness. Stillness is not weakness. Sometimes they are the body's oldest forms of wisdom.

When emotional unpredictability surrounds a child, the body adapts long before the mind understands what it is adapting to.
Stillness becomes strategy.
Softness becomes camouflage.
Quiet becomes survival.

Not because the child is passive — but because the child is wise.

This chapter explores how fear shapes nervous systems, how stillness becomes self-protection, and how what once guarded survival later matures into intuition, empathy, and healing.

THE FEAR ATMOSPHERE

Fear is not always loud.
Sometimes it is the heavy silence in a room…
the subtle shift in a parent's breath…
the tension that gathers before words do.

Children do not require explanations to feel unsafe.
They feel emotional pressure immediately.

When a child senses that the emotional climate can change without warning, the nervous system begins to stay primed:

- alert,
- cautious,
- attuned to tone,
- sensitive to tension,
- preparing for the next shift.

This is what psychologists call limbic surveillance — the instinct to constantly scan the environment for danger.

Many adults who grew up in unpredictable emotional spaces still do this today:

- they anticipate reactions,
- overthink before speaking,
- watch others closely,
- and adjust themselves based on who is in the room.

It begins as survival.
It later looks like empathy.

But its roots are in the atmosphere of childhood fear.

EMOTIONAL INSTABILITY

Adult chaos, stress, or unprocessed wounds echo into the emotional world of a child.

When the emotional stability of caregivers fluctuates without explanation, the child's worldview forms around uncertainty:

- "I must be ready at all times."
- "Anything could change suddenly."
- "I have to make myself small to avoid conflict."

- "I must be careful not to upset anyone."
- "I am responsible for keeping peace."

Even when a child is not the cause of emotional instability, they often feel responsible for calming it.

They learn to regulate themselves — not to find inner peace, but to avoid triggering others.

This internal regulation later appears as:

- politeness,
- diplomacy,
- restraint,
- emotional maturity,
- sensitivity to injustice,
- and remarkable empathy.

The shadow child becomes the emotionally intelligent adult.

But the price at the time was vigilance.

FREEZING, OBSERVING, DISAPPEARING

The human body has four ancient instinctive reactions to threat:

- fight
- flight
- freeze
- fawn

For many sensitive children, freeze becomes the safest option.

Freezing has many forms:

- going quiet

- shrinking inside
- not making eye contact
- holding the breath
- numbing emotions
- pretending to sleep
- staying very still
- becoming invisible

In adulthood, the same response appears as:

- shutting down during conflict
- dissociating in stressful moments
- going numb instead of emotional
- losing your voice when overwhelmed
- retreating inward when hurt

Freezing is not weakness.
It is intelligence.

It is the body's way of surviving a situation that cannot be escaped or resolved.

Observing is the same.

Children who cannot intervene learn to watch instead:

- studying relationships
- noticing tone changes
- reading emotional signals
- detecting when something is "off"
- remembering patterns others never saw

Disappearing is also an instinct.

It is the emotional version of camouflage.

When presence feels risky, invisibility feels safe.

These responses shape how a child learns to move through the world.

They also shape how that child later becomes:

- highly intuitive,
- spiritually perceptive,
- empathetic,
- tuned to energy,
- and gifted at sensing emotional truth.

WHY INTUITION DEVELOPS EARLY

Many intuitives, healers, and sensitives were trained by childhood.

Not through books, meditation, or spiritual rituals...

...but through emotional necessity.

To stay safe, the child had to:

- feel danger before it arrived
- scan the emotional field
- interpret body language
- sense tension without being told
- hear what wasn't spoken
- anticipate reactions
- understand moods instantly

This sensory awareness is the foundation of intuitive intelligence.

Children who grow up needing to decode the emotional world become adults who:

- instantly sense discomfort

- detect dishonesty
- feel emotional pain in others
- anticipate unspoken needs
- hold space naturally
- offer comfort without being asked

Intuition is not mystical in its origin.

It is survival sharpened into insight.

When life requires you to stay aware, the body learns to read energy instead of language.

Later, when life becomes safer, that same capacity becomes a gift.

What once felt like hyper-awareness transforms into empathy, sensitivity, and wisdom.

THE SEEDS OF THE HEALER

Here is the paradox few understand:

The same qualities that were born to protect you are the ones that now allow you to help others.

The child who learned to stay quiet becomes the adult who listens deeply.
The child who learned to sense emotional storms becomes the adult who intuitively guides others through theirs.
The child who learned to observe becomes the adult who sees the soul.
The child who learned to survive becomes the adult who teaches healing.

Many healers did not choose their path.
Their path began forming in silence, during childhood moments
of uncertainty.

Sensitivity, awareness, compassion, discernment, intuition —
these were not hobbies.

They were survival skills.

And over time, survival skills became spiritual gifts.

You learned to hold energy.
You learned to transmute fear.
You learned to stay calm in emotional storms.
You learned to feel what others could not articulate.
You learned to protect those more vulnerable than you.

These are the seeds of the healer.

Some people arrive at healing through study.
Others arrive because their childhood trained their nervous
system to walk between shadow and light.

They know what fear feels like.
They know what silence feels like.
And they know what it means to witness — and survive —
emotional darkness.

That is why they become the light for others.

Healing, for them, is not a profession.

It is the natural evolution of who they were forced to become.

IN TRUTH...

Stillness was never a flaw.
Quiet was never weakness.
Sensitivity was never fragility.

They were the body's earliest forms of wisdom.

If you grew up learning to freeze, observe, stay small, or become invisible...

it was because your system was brilliant, adaptive, and determined to keep you safe.

And now, as an adult, you are invited to meet that younger self and say:

*"Thank you for protecting me.
Your job is done now.
I can take it from here."*

The shadow begins to heal when the stillness no longer needs to hide.

Because stillness, when safe, transforms into clarity.

Observation becomes intuition.
Sensitivity becomes compassion.
And the quiet child becomes the healer.

CHAPTER 6 — The Day the Shadow Broke Open

There is always a moment when a child realizes that something is not normal — not because anyone explained it, but because the body knew before the mind could name it.

Every shadow has an origin point.

Not necessarily the moment fear first arrived,
but the moment the child saw fear clearly.

A moment when the atmosphere shifted from confusion into recognition.

For some, that moment is silent.
For others, it is sudden and loud.
For many, it is a single experience that splits childhood into "before" and "after."

For me, it happened in a crowded room on an ordinary day.

THE EXPLOSIVE MOMENT

Family had gathered.
Laughter, conversation, plates, food, voices — a normal scene layered with warmth and familiarity.

And then, without warning, the air changed.

Tension swept through the room like a storm forming without clouds.
Voices sharpened.
Energy rose.
Silence collapsed.

And the table fell — lifted, thrown, or struck in a burst of anger that felt larger than the room itself.

Chairs scattered.
Children stunned.
Eyes wide, breath shallow.

In that instant, something inside me split:

Before that moment, I believed the atmosphere I lived in was just "how life was."
After that moment, I understood that what I felt wasn't normal — it was unsafe.

It is often a single dramatic event that gives shape to everything our intuition has sensed in fragments.

The child sees:

"This is real.
This is not my imagination.
This is not my fault."

The shadow breaks open not from fear itself, but from clarity.

LEAVING THE UNSAFE PARENT

That day became a turning point for my family.

Decisions were made quietly, but with weight:

- a separation,
- distance,
- a choosing of safety over tolerance,
- a boundary drawn not with words but with action.

For a child, leaving an unsafe parent is not simple to understand.

It can feel confusing, disorienting, heartbreaking.
A child may long for the parent even while knowing instinctively that distance is protection.

Yet even in the confusion, something profound begins:

A child who once felt powerless learns that change is possible.
A child who once believed emotional danger must be endured discovers that safety can be chosen.
A child who once assumed fear was normal begins to question that belief.

Leaving the unsafe environment became the first act of reclaiming my nervous system.

Not because I understood it fully,
but because my body felt it instantly.

The emotional air became lighter.

The threat became quieter.

I learned what it meant for the body to feel safe.

Perhaps for the first time.

THE FIRST BREATH OF SAFETY

When you live in an emotional storm long enough, calm feels unfamiliar.

But the body knows it.

When the environment shifted, I remember a physical change — not intellectual, not verbal, not logical.

A single breath that was different from all the breaths before.

Relief.
Space.
Quiet that didn't feel dangerous.
Stillness without tension.
A sense that my shoulders could drop, even slightly.

That was my first somatic experience of safety.

Safety is not a concept.
It is a body sensation.

It feels like:

- breathing without bracing,
- existing without shrinking,
- speaking without fear,
- being present without calculating.

Most children who grow up in fear don't realize they're afraid until they experience a place where fear is absent.

For me, that breath became a reference point — a blueprint.

From that moment on, I knew what safe felt like.

And whether I understood it consciously or not, that feeling would become the compass that guided every healing choice I made later.

THE BEGINNING OF CLARITY

When children experience fear long enough, they normalize it.

But when the shadow breaks open — when an event draws the unseen into the visible — the child begins to see patterns:

- emotional volatility
- instability
- disrespect
- tension
- unpredictability

The table flipping was not the beginning of pain.

It was the beginning of awareness.

A moment of inner truth that said:

"This is not how love looks."

That moment — and the leaving that followed — set in motion the slow evolution of the healer within me.

Because clarity births questions:

Why did I feel unsafe?
Why did I work so hard to be small?
Why did I sense danger before anyone spoke?

Why did silence feel safer than expression?
Why did emotional energy determine my behaviour?

These were not questions I asked as a child.

But they took root that day.

And decades later, they became the foundation of my work:

- helping others understand their fear,
- teaching them how emotional imprints form,
- guiding them toward their own clarity,
- showing them what safety feels like,
- helping them release shadows born in silence.

When the shadow cracks, the light begins to seep through.

The moment something collapses is often the moment something inside begins.

In that childhood scene — emotional pressure rising, objects crashing, decisions unfolding — I learned something powerful:

The shadow is not made from what happened.

It is made from what we believed about ourselves because of what happened.

And that belief can change.

I did not walk away from childhood with clarity.
But I walked away with a truth that my body carried for years:

I was never meant to live in fear.
And I would one day help others leave it behind, too.

CHAPTER 7 — The Trip That Revealed the Truth

There comes a moment when the child inside us stops absorbing the world... and begins interpreting it. A moment when survival turns into awareness.

There are events in childhood that settle into the body quietly — unnamed, half-remembered, and blurry around the edges.
We may not fully understand them at the time, but something inside us recognizes a shift.

For me, that moment arrived far from home, during a trip that was meant to be ordinary.

It was there that I first realized danger was real — not imagined, not misinterpreted — and that the same intuitive skills that once made me silent could, in the right moment, become courage.

REALIZING DANGER

Children do not always understand what is happening around them, but they recognize when something is wrong.

During that trip, I noticed:

- boundaries that did not feel right,
- behavior that didn't match safety,
- a tension in the air that felt familiar,
- and a power dynamic that made my instincts rise.

I didn't have adult language.
I didn't have explanations.
I didn't have proof.

But I had my body.
And my body felt unsafe.

That was the first time I consciously realized:

Fear is not always mine—sometimes it is a signal.

Up until then, I had absorbed fear like oxygen.

This was the moment I began to *recognize* it.

Recognition is often the first step in breaking generational patterns.

FINDING COURAGE

Courage rarely arrives with confidence.
It usually arrives through instinct.

In that moment, something awakened in me:

- a boundary,
- a refusal,
- a pushback against what once felt inevitable.

When the situation crossed the line between discomfort and threat, the child inside me shifted from silent witness to protector.

I physically pulled away.
I created distance.

I corrected the moment with the only body language I knew:
No.

It was messy, imperfect, impulsive, and powerful.

That act — small as it was — became a declaration:

"I will not surrender my safety."

Children are often taught to obey, to be polite, to go along, to minimize themselves.

But when the shadow is threatened, it also becomes the spark:

- of instinct,
- of resistance,
- of self-protection.

That spark is the seed of self-worth.

And it lives in every child who ever sensed danger and moved away from it.

SPEAKING UP

Later, when the unease continued, I did something I had never done before:

I spoke.

I shared what happened.
I named what I felt.
I trusted my intuition more than my silence.

For a child who learned that disappearance meant safety, speaking is a form of rebellion.

It is also an act of self-love.

When the truth finally surfaced, it did not stay with me.
It rippled outward.

Someone else spoke, too.
Someone else was freed from the silence they had been
carrying.

This is how shadows dissolve:

One voice becomes two.
Two voices become protection.
Truth breaks the isolation that fear builds around children.

Speaking isn't always loud.
Sometimes it is an unsteady sentence or a trembling confession.

But every time a child speaks their truth, a chain breaks.

PROTECTING OTHERS

One of the most powerful things about shadow-born intuition is
that it doesn't only protect the self — it protects others.

In that moment, I not only recognized danger for me...
I recognized it for other children.

I felt responsibility, not out of guilt but out of empathy.

I saw what silence could allow.
I saw what speaking could prevent.

That instinct — the one that moved me to speak, to warn, to
protect — became the foundation of who I would later become:

Someone who advocates for others,
someone who sees what others overlook,
someone who steps forward when silence endangers innocence.

Many healers carry this same trait:

Their earliest courage wasn't used to defend themselves —
it was used to protect someone else.

That is the heart of empathy.

Born from shadow.
Transformed into service.

THE MOMENT LIFE CHANGED DIRECTION

After that trip, nothing looked the same.

Truth came into focus.
Family patterns cracked open.
Secrets were faced.
Boundaries were drawn.

There was grief in the clarity.
There was fear in the honesty.
There was disruption in the unraveling.

But there was also freedom.

For me, it was the moment childhood ended — not because I
"grew up," but because I understood something that could no
longer be unlearned:

Human behavior is not always safe.
And intuition is often the first warning.

From that day forward, I trusted:

- what I sensed,
- what my body told me,
- what atmosphere revealed,
- and what silence tried to hide.

Years later, as an adult, as a healer, as someone who works with the emotional body...

I look back on that moment not as the source of pain, but as the beginning of awareness.

It is when I first understood that the inner child is not naive — they are perceptive.

And I honor that child for feeling what I could not yet name.

For resisting what felt wrong.
For speaking when silence was expected.
For protecting others with instincts that were wiser than their years.

That moment did not define me.
It guided me.

It did not break me.
It revealed me.

It showed me the path I was meant to walk —
a path that would one day help others recognize danger, trust intuition, break silence, and choose safety.

For it is often the day the shadow cracks...

that a new, brighter version of the self begins.

CHAPTER 8 — When the Past Tested Me Again

Healing is not always a straight line. Sometimes life returns to test the strength of the voice we once didn't have.

Becoming a mother changes the architecture of the heart.

It awakens instincts that were always present but never fully realized.
It expands awareness beyond self-protection and into something fierce, sacred, and immovable:

the protection of the innocent.

Motherhood often brings the past into sharper focus.
Not as memory, but as comparison.

When I held my child, I understood something my younger self never could:

The atmosphere I grew up in was not normal.
And it was not acceptable.

That realization became the foundation of my courage.

BECOMING A MOTHER

When my daughter entered the world, she arrived untouched by fear or silence.

She was pure possibility.
Unmarked by instability.
Beautifully unaware of the emotional complexity that shaped me.

Looking at her, I felt two truths at the same time:

- Awe at her innocence
- And a firm, unshakable vow that she would never carry the shadows I carried

Motherhood called forward a new identity.

Not the quiet child.
Not the silent observer.
Not the frozen watcher.

But the protector.

The woman who would stand between her child and anything that resembled the world she once endured.

Motherhood did not reopen old wounds —
it gave them purpose.

FACING THE PAST WITH STRENGTH

Years passed, and life moved forward.
The distance from my childhood brought clarity, healing, and strength.

But then, the past came knocking again.

Literally.

The person who had once been unsafe reappeared at my door —
no longer just a shadow from memory, but a physical presence standing on my threshold, accompanied by a woman and her two daughters.

There are moments when instinct speaks louder than fear ever did.

I didn't tremble.
I didn't shrink.
I didn't freeze.

The child in me once stayed silent.
But the woman had grown.

I welcomed the woman and her children because they needed shelter.
But I did not surrender my awareness.

I paid attention.
I noticed patterns.
I felt the atmosphere.
And when intuition confirmed what I already knew — that these children were now in danger — I stepped forward.

I faced the past not as a wounded child,
but as an adult with conviction.

PROTECTING CHILDREN

Protecting a child is sacred work — whether they are your own, or simply under your roof.

When I discovered that he had begun targeting one of the girls, instinct and clarity merged.

I spoke the truth out loud.
I brought light into a place that tried to hide in shadow.
I told their mother.

Once again, the moment of speaking became a crack in the silence.

No shaking.
No fear that telling the truth would bring harm.
Just clarity.

I was no longer the little girl who froze in fear.
I was the woman who confronted the storm.

And when his anger rose, I did not cower.

Counseling, healing, spiritual work, and growth had changed my foundation.
I was no longer shaped by fear.
I was informed by it.

And that difference matters.

The woman I had become stood between children and the person who once stood between safety and me.

That is what breaking a cycle looks like.

GOING TO THE POLICE

Truth needs to be spoken.
But sometimes, it also needs structure.

I brought what I knew to the authorities.
Not to seek revenge.
Not from anger.
But from responsibility.

Even though much of what happened in my childhood could not
be proven in a courtroom — my voice mattered.

Years passed, and others came forward.
And when the time came for the system to take action, my
previous testimony helped form a bigger picture.

The silence that once protected harm now helped protect
children.

Sometimes justice does not look like punishment —
sometimes it is simply truth finally landing where it should.

BECOMING THE CYCLE-BREAKER

There is a moment in every healer's journey when the past
returns — not to wound, but to test.

And the test is simple:

Are you who you used to be...
or who you have become?

When the past stood at my doorstep, I recognized myself in a
way I never fully had before.

I was not the frozen child.
I was not the silent observer.
I was not the girl who blamed herself for what she didn't understand.

I was the adult who could see clearly.
The woman who could speak.
The mother who protected.
The counselor who understood patterns.
The healer who recognized shadows.
The cycle-breaker who would not pass fear forward to the next generation.

My daughter would not inherit the silence I once lived with.
And neither would other children, if I could help it.

To break a cycle is not to hate the past.
It is to refuse to repeat it.

It is choosing:

- safety over secrecy,
- truth over denial,
- courage over silence,
- protection over comfort,
- and clarity over confusion.

Becoming a cycle-breaker does not happen in a single moment.
It is lived, step by step, voice by voice, decision by decision.

And for many of us, it begins the moment the past tries to come back…

and finds that we are no longer the same person it once shaped.

That is when shadow truly shifts into light.

CHAPTER 9 — The Woman Who Emerged

Healing is not about returning to who you were before the storm — it is about becoming who you were designed to be because of it.

Not every child who grows up in shadow becomes trapped by it.
Some rise through it.
Some build their lives around truth, protection, insight, and service.

From the outside, it may look like resilience.
On the inside, it is simply the natural unfoldment of a nervous system trained to understand the human heart.

This chapter marks the turning point — the transition from survivor to seeker, from silence to wisdom, from watcher to healer.

SELF-AWARENESS

As time passed and adulthood unfolded, I began to notice something important:

I wasn't reacting to life the way others did.

I sensed things that weren't spoken.
I paid attention to subtleties others overlooked.

I carried emotional insight that did not come from books.
I noticed atmospheres before conversations began.

And I asked questions most people never thought to ask:

- Why do we feel certain emotions without knowing why?
- Why do bodies react before minds understand?
- How do childhood experiences shape adult relationships, fears, and beliefs?
- What does safety feel like in the body?
- What is intuition, and where does it come from?

Self-awareness wasn't an achievement —
it was the natural evolution of a childhood spent in emotional observation.

The same sensitivity that once helped me survive became the key to understanding myself.

Instead of fearing my patterns, I studied them.
Instead of shaming my reactions, I became curious.
Instead of blaming the child I once was, I embraced her as the beginning of all my gifts.

Self-awareness became freedom.

INTUITION SHARPENED BY SURVIVAL

Growing up attuned to emotional shifts creates a kind of inner radar.

Some call it intuition.
Some call it empathy.
Some call it spiritual sensing.

It is all three.

The emotional vigilance that once protected me began to transform into wisdom:

- I could sense when someone needed comfort.
- I could read the emotional roots beneath words.
- I could feel energy in spaces.
- I could recognize people's wounds before they spoke of them.
- I could tell when someone's anger was actually fear, or when silence was actually pain.

These abilities no longer came from hypervigilance.
They came from clarity, compassion, and understanding.

Survival shaped the instrument.
Healing refined the sound.

And intuition became a gift — one I would later use in teaching, guiding, practicing spiritual work, and helping others navigate their own shadows.

This is how many healers are formed:

First, they learn how to read the world.
Then, they learn how to reshape it.

HEALING THROUGH LEARNING

I did not stay in silence.

I sought answers — not only for my past, but for my purpose.

I pursued counseling.
I studied human behavior.
I explored healing practices.
I learned the language of the nervous system.

I worked with mentors, teachers, modalities, traditions, and spiritual systems.

The more I learned, the lighter my shadow became.

Education offered clarity.
Understanding offered compassion.
Spiritual study offered peace.

Knowledge did not erase the past.
It explained it.

And once I understood the emotional architecture of my childhood, I could dismantle what no longer served me.

Learning became healing.

Not because it removed pain, but because it untangled confusion.

FINDING MEANING

There is a stage in healing when the story shifts from:

"Why did this happen to me?"
to
"What has this given me?"

For me, the answers were profound:

- emotional intelligence
- empathy
- compassion
- intuition
- courage
- discernment
- resilience

- strength
- spiritual depth
- the desire to prevent harm
- the ability to hold space for others

The shadow did not break me.
It shaped the exact qualities I would need for my life's work.

It made me attentive to suffering.
It made me intuitive to silence.
It made me protective of innocence.
It made me see beyond masks and words.

And slowly, I began to feel a deeper truth rising inside me:

What once threatened to silence me had instead prepared me to guide others out of silence.

Meaning grows where wounds are met with understanding.

And the past becomes sacred when it gives us purpose.

THE BEGINNING OF YOUR CALLING

Some people search their whole lives for their calling.

Others are shaped by it long before they realize it exists.

Long before I taught, practiced, wrote, or guided, the path was already forming:

- in every moment I sensed emotional tension
- in every instinct that warned me of danger
- in every step I took toward safety
- in every word I spoke to protect others
- in every question I asked about healing

- in every hour spent learning how the human spirit restores itself

My calling did not come from books.
It rose from the child who survived by reading the emotional world.

It came from the stillness that taught me to listen.
From the complexity that taught me compassion.
From the silence that taught me truth.
From the shadows that taught me light.

When the past came to my door years later, and I met it without fear, I finally understood:

I was not here to be the one who stayed silent —
I was here to become the one who speaks, teaches, protects, heals, and shines.

Everything that once felt heavy became material for transformation.

Every shadow that once felt threatening became a doorway.

Every moment of confusion became a skill.
Every fear became a compass.
Every silence became intuition.
Every crack became light.

This is the woman who emerged:

Not defined by what she endured —
but shaped by what she overcame.

Not carrying darkness —
but carrying wisdom.

Not trapped by the past —
but called by the future.

And that calling, once just a whisper, became unshakable:

To help others find their voice.
To guide others through their shadows.
To walk beside those who are ready to reclaim the light they
were born with.

This was the beginning.

Not of pain —
but of purpose.

Not of wounds —
but of service.

Not of fear —
but of a lifelong devotion to healing.

And from that moment forward, every step would lead deeper
into the work my soul had been preparing for since childhood:

The work of helping others come home to themselves.

SECTION III — THE SHADOW HEALING PROCESS

CHAPTER 10 — Meeting Your Shadow with Compassion

The shadow does not demand correction — it asks for understanding.

Before we go deeper into shadow healing, we must establish something essential:

You cannot shame, force, or judge your shadow into light.

Healing is not punishment.
It is a reunion.

This chapter introduces the mindset that allows integration to happen safely: compassion, gentleness, and emotional truth.

Because that is where real transformation begins.

THE DIFFERENCE BETWEEN TRUTH AND IDENTITY

One of the great mistakes people make in shadow work is confusing:

- what happened
  with
- who they are

Childhood experiences can create powerful emotional beliefs:

- "I am unsafe"
- "I am unworthy"
- "I cause problems"
- "I am invisible"
- "I must stay small"
- "My feelings are dangerous"

But these beliefs are not identity.
They are interpretations — conclusions formed by a child who tried to make sense of an environment bigger than they were.

Truth is this:

Your shadow is not you — it is the version of you that formed when you were trying to survive.

Identity is who you became when you had safety, maturity, choice, voice, autonomy, and self-awareness.

Shadow beliefs are emotional echoes of the past.
They are the nervous system's attempt to make meaning out of confusion.

Shadow work invites you to separate the two:

Truth:
"I experienced emotional instability."

Identity:
"I am resilient, intuitive, and aware because I survived it."

Truth:
"As a child, I learned silence as protection."

Identity:
"As an adult, I choose when to speak, how to share, and
who I am safe with."

When people heal, they are not "changing who they are" —
they are releasing the identities that were never theirs to begin
with.

GENTLE ACKNOWLEDGMENT

The shadow formed to protect you.
For many people, it was an intelligent and necessary tool.

That is why the first step in healing is not confrontation.

It is acknowledgment.

Gentle acknowledgment sounds like:

- "I understand why I reacted the way I did."
- "I see why my younger self stayed quiet."
- "I know why I learned to expect danger."
- "I can feel the moment fear took root."
- "I don't blame myself for surviving the way I had to."

When you meet the shadow with gentleness —
the nervous system relaxes.
The inner child begins to breathe.
The protective patterns soften.

The shadow is not made of darkness.
It is made of misunderstood emotion.

When it feels seen, it becomes less reactive.

Many people fear their shadow because they believe it is chaotic.
But it becomes chaotic only when ignored, denied, judged, or shoved back down.

When approached with compassion, the shadow reveals the truth of how you became who you are:

- what you protected,
- what you needed,
- what you feared,
- and what you did not yet understand.

Acknowledgment is not weakness.
It is partnership with your own soul.

WHY HARSH SELF-JUDGMENT BLOCKS HEALING

The shadow is already carrying the weight of:

- confusion,
- fear,
- shame,
- misinterpretation,
- responsibility that wasn't yours,
- and beliefs that were never true.

Adding judgment on top of that does not heal —
it retraumatizes.

Harsh self-judgment says:

- "I should be over this by now."
- "I'm weak because I still react."
- "Something is wrong with me."
- "I should not feel this way."

But the nervous system does not respond to force.
It responds to safety.

Judgment tells the shadow,
"You are wrong for existing."

Compassion tells it,
"You make sense. You did your best. And now we can grow beyond this."

Healing cannot happen in a hostile environment — even a silent, internal one.

Self-judgment traps the shadow in survival mode.
Compassion invites the shadow into integration.

Because when you soften toward yourself, you say:

"I am safe now.
And everything I once hid is welcome to return."

THE HEART OF SHADOW HEALING

Shadow work is not about:

- excavating every detail,
- reliving pain,
- or demanding perfection.

It is about gently recognizing the parts of yourself that were once alone.

The goal is wholeness —
to allow every version of you to exist in the same heart, without shame.

There is a simple truth at the core of this work:

Everything you hid was trying to protect you.
And everything you hid deserves love as it comes back into the light.

When you meet your shadow with compassion, you begin to dissolve fear.
When you separate truth from identity, you begin to restore your inner sovereignty.
When you release judgment, you allow self-acceptance to take root.

This is the doorway into deeper healing.

And from here, you no longer see the shadow as an enemy…

but as the guardian that held your light until you were ready to reclaim it.

CHAPTER 11 — The Four Shadow Archetypes

The Silent Child

The one who learned that safety lived in silence.

Some shadows speak loudly through anger, rebellion, or resistance.

Others express themselves through quiet — a subtle shrinking, a careful stillness, a soft voice that carries more wisdom than the child could ever say.

The Silent Child is not quiet by nature.
They became quiet by need.

Their silence was their shield, their protection, their survival code.

This chapter explores how the Silent Child forms, how they move through adulthood, and how that silence can be transformed into clarity, voice, and healed expression.

HOW THE SILENT CHILD IS BORN

Not all children speak when something feels wrong.

Some learn early that drawing attention brings danger.

This child discovers that being quiet works:

- If I stay small, there is less conflict.
- If I don't ask questions, I won't be scolded.
- If I don't react, maybe the storm will pass.
- If I disappear a little, no one will be upset.
- If I hold my breath, maybe everything will go back to normal.

Silence becomes a form of emotional camouflage.

Not out of obedience.
But out of intelligence.

The Silent Child understands, even without language, that their voice cannot change the atmosphere around them — but silence might help them survive it.

They watch.
They listen.
They wait.
They stay out of the way.

Silence becomes the sacred space where they can exist without drawing danger closer.

THE INNER RULES OF THE SILENT CHILD

Without ever being told directly, they adopt beliefs that shape how they speak, feel, and behave:

- "I must not say too much."
- "I should not show emotion."
- "If I stay quiet, nothing bad will happen."
- "Nobody wants to hear what I think."
- "My needs will upset others."
- "Speaking makes me unsafe."
- "It is easier to carry things alone."

These beliefs may have kept them safe once.

But they often follow the person into adulthood — long after silence is no longer required.

THE SILENT CHILD IN THE ADULT BODY

You can recognize traces of this archetype in adults who:

- struggle to express needs
- avoid asking for help
- minimize their emotions
- hesitate to speak their truth
- feel guilt for taking up space
- worry that their feelings are "too much"
- withdraw during conflict
- default to "I'm fine" even when hurt
- silence themselves to prevent discomfort in others

Their voice is not gone.
It was simply tucked away.

For many, expression feels unsafe even when their reality is safe.

They do not fear speaking —
they fear consequences they once believed silence prevented.

The Silent Child still sits at the edge of their communication, whispering:

*"Careful.
We've been here before."*

WHY THE SILENT CHILD IS NOT BROKEN

Many adults shame themselves for their silence.

They call it weakness, insecurity, or emotional immaturity.

But silence that once ensured survival is not a flaw.

It is brilliance.

It is the proof that the child saw and understood more than anyone realized.

While other children spoke freely, they observed emotional truth.

While others asked questions, they read the room.

While others rushed forward, they sensed invisible danger.

Silence is not emptiness.

It is awareness held inward.

And the Silent Child grew into someone who knows:

- what someone means, even when they deny it
- when an atmosphere is tense, before anyone reacts
- when another person is drowning inside their own silence

This empathy is not accidental.

It is shadow-born wisdom.

WHEN SILENCE BECOMES A WOUND

Silence becomes painful in adulthood when it begins to limit growth:

When someone longs to speak truth, but freezes.
When emotions pile up behind the ribs, unexpressed.
When needs are never voiced.
When a person abandons their own voice to preserve peace.

The Silent Child may become the adult who apologizes for speaking at all —
or who feels invisible in relationships because they don't know how to express what they truly feel.

Their silence is not stubbornness.
It is conditioning.

It is the nervous system protecting them from memories of danger that no longer exist.

HOW SILENCE BEGINS TO HEAL

The Silent Child does not need loudness to heal.

They do not need to suddenly speak boldly, or shout, or demand.

Healing begins with small internal permissions:

- "It is safe for me to speak."
- "My feelings matter."

- "My voice has value."
- "I can express emotion without harm."
- "I deserve to be heard."

Healing silence is not about volume.
It is about safety.

It is helping the nervous system understand that:

Expression is no longer dangerous.

For some, the first step is whispering their truth to themselves.
For others, it is speaking vulnerably to one trusted person.
For many, journaling becomes their first voice.

The goal is not noise.

The goal is authenticity.

THE GIFT OF THE SILENT CHILD

When healed, the Silent Child becomes:

- a powerful communicator
- a wise listener
- someone who speaks truth with precision
- someone whose words land deeply
- someone others feel safe around
- someone who understands pauses, emotions, tears, and silence in others

Their voice carries weight because they speak from observation rather than reaction.

Their empathy is deep because they know what it feels like to be unseen.

Their intuition is strong because they spent years reading the emotional energy beneath words.

And their compassion is profound because they once learned to carry everything inward.

The Silent Child is not meant to disappear.

They are meant to become someone who speaks truth when it matters most.

THE RECLAMATION

At some point, the adult self must turn inward and meet the silent child with gentleness:

"You kept me safe.
Your silence protected me.
But I can speak now.
And I want you to be free."

This moment is sacred.

It is where shadow becomes integration.

It is the first breath of voice returning.

And the beginning of expression that is not forced —
but chosen.

The Silent Child never needed to be loud.

They simply needed to believe they were safe to speak.

Because their voice was never the problem.

It was simply waiting for the moment the heart was strong enough to carry its truth.

And when that happens —
their quiet wisdom becomes courage.

Their silence becomes clarity.

Their presence becomes light.

And the shadow they once held becomes the foundation of everything they will ever heal in themselves and others.

The Watcher

The one who learned to see everything, because not seeing felt unsafe.

Some children develop silence as a shield.
Others develop awareness as strategy.

The Watcher is the child whose safety depended on emotional prediction — someone who needed to anticipate shifts, moods, and dangers before they arrived.

The Watcher is not paranoid.

They are perceptive.

They do not wait for problems to become obvious.

They feel them building in the atmosphere.

Hyper-awareness was their armor — a skill they mastered long before they knew it had a name.

HOW THE WATCHER IS FORMED

The Watcher emerges in environments where emotional instability feels unpredictable or confusing.

When a child senses:

- rapid changes in tone,
- unexpected reactions,
- anger without warning,
- stress too heavy for their age,
- emotional chaos,
- secrets,

- painful silence,
- or tension that was never explained...

They begin scanning the world continuously.

They watch everything:

- body language,
- footsteps,
- expressions,
- patterns,
- emotional changes,
- energy shifts,
- unspoken meanings.

The Watcher listens between sentences.
They track what others can't see.
They notice things that adults overlook.

Their nervous system is always slightly ahead of the moment:

*"What is coming next?
And how do I prepare for it?"*

This is not fear-based, although it begins in fear.
It becomes instinct — sharpened over years.

THE INTERNAL RULES OF THE WATCHER

Without ever being taught, these beliefs shape the Watcher's world:

- "Safety depends on my awareness."
- "I need to stay alert at all times."
- "I must detect danger before it arrives."

- "If I can read people well enough, I won't be blindsided."
- "Predicting emotions keeps me safe."

Their attention is constantly tuned to the emotional wavelength around them.

Even as adults, many Watchers sit with their back to the wall in restaurants, scan faces during conversations, or feel the emotional climate of a room before their coat is even off.

They do not do this by choice.

Their nervous system learned it before memory existed.

THE WATCHER IN THE ADULT BODY

In adulthood, Watchers often appear:

- calm,
- insightful,
- empathetic,
- emotionally intelligent,
- intuitive to patterns,
- excellent at reading people,
- highly skilled at conflict avoidance and de-escalation.

They are the ones who sense tension before voices even change pitch.

They notice shifts even when someone says "I'm fine."

They feel when someone is lying, withholding, or in pain.

Watchers can seem quiet or reserved from the outside, but internally they are scanning layers:

- emotions,
- intentions,
- energetic signals,
- micro-expressions,
- tone changes,
- subtle discomforts.

They listen deeply and see clearly.

But they rarely reveal how much they know.

THE SHADOW SIDE OF HYPER-AWARENESS

Awareness is a gift — but it can also become exhausting.

When the Watcher stays in survival mode, hyper-awareness creates:

- anxiety,
- sensitivity to conflict,
- emotional exhaustion,
- fear of unpredictability,
- difficulty resting,
- trouble trusting,
- over-responsibility for others' moods.

Many Watchers feel uncomfortable when they can't "read the room" — or if they sense emotional signals that don't align with what is being said.

Their body remembers when unpredictability meant danger.

So they watch instinctively, even when danger no longer exists.

WHEN WATCHING BECOMES A GIFT

When healed, Watchers become:

- exceptional listeners
- intuitive guides
- counselors
- energy workers
- protectors
- mediators
- wise observers
- truth detectors
- emotionally safe leaders

They see what sits beneath the surface.

They help others feel understood without explaining.

They recognize when someone is hurting before the person speaks.

They notice:

- the tremor in a voice,
- the way someone's eyes drop at the word "love,"
- the pause between sentences when something is unspoken,
- the shift in posture that reveals insecurity,
- the way silence thickens when a wound is touched.

This sensitivity is not a flaw.

It's a spiritual instrument.

One that took years to refine.

WHY INTUITION WAS BORN THROUGH WATCHING

Hyper-awareness teaches the brain how to track energy, not words.

Watchers learned to:

- interpret emotional currents,
- decode unspoken messages,
- sense truth behind facades,
- recognize danger without "evidence,"
- pick up on subtle patterns in behavior.

These same abilities later appear as:

- clair-sentience
- intuitive knowing
- strong empathy
- spiritual sensitivity
- healing insight

Many who grow up as Watchers become natural energy healers because the skill they mastered as children — reading the unseen — is the same skill required to sense subtle shifts in aura, thought, belief, and emotion.

They became intuitive not through mysticism…

but through necessity.

HOW THE WATCHER HEALS

The Watcher heals not by losing awareness
but by learning safety.

When the nervous system recognizes that threats no longer
exist, vigilance slows, softens, relaxes.

Healing begins with statements like:

- "I am safe now."
- "I do not need to stay alert at all times."
- "I can notice without bracing."
- "Awareness is a gift, not a burden."
- "My intuition is not fear — it is wisdom."

The goal is not to suppress perception —
it is to release the belief that awareness is required for survival.

Once fear dissolves, awareness becomes insight.
Observation becomes intuition.
Vigilance becomes clarity.

The Watcher stops scanning for threat and begins noticing
beauty.

The same eyes that once searched for danger learn to search for
truth, connection, synchronicity, and meaning.

The presence that once protected becomes presence that heals.

THE GIFT OF THE WATCHER

Watchers are often the ones who:

- sense emotional needs
- prevent unnecessary harm
- hold safe space
- understand grief
- detect manipulation
- honor vulnerability
- comfort quietly

- speak truth carefully
- guide others gently

They know what suffering looks like — even when hidden.
They know what silence feels like — even when disguised as strength.

Their awareness, when integrated, becomes wisdom.

Their vigilance becomes discernment.
Their sensitivity becomes intuition.
Their observation becomes empathy.
Their insight becomes guidance.

The Watcher, healed and whole, is one of the most powerful healers on earth.

Because they learned from the shadows how to see light.

The Protector

The one who learned to carry responsibility that never belonged to them.

Some children go silent.
Some become watchful.

And others take on a third role:

They become Protector.

These are the children who step into emotional roles far beyond their years — caretakers, mediators, peacekeepers, rescuers, nurturers, and shields.

They learned to quiet storms, to make others feel better, to soften chaos, and to absorb pain that was not theirs.

The Protector did not become responsible because they wanted to.

They became responsible because someone had to be.

HOW THE PROTECTOR IS FORMED

This archetype appears when a child senses instability, emotional fragility, or the absence of safety in their environment.

They feel the weight of unspoken fear or confusion and instinctively step forward.

They might:

- comfort a distressed parent

- soothe a sibling
- keep secrets
- smooth tension
- anticipate triggers
- absorb blame
- offer emotional support

They do not say:

"I'll handle this."

They simply do.

Because something inside them knows:

"If I help, maybe everything will stay calm."

For a child, this is not strategy —
it is survival through empathy.

They become emotional caretakers long before they understand
what the role costs.

THE INTERNAL RULES OF THE PROTECTOR

Most Protectors absorb beliefs that shape their sense of
responsibility:

- "I must take care of others."
- "Their pain is my job to fix."
- "I have to prevent conflict."
- "I should not upset anyone."
- "If I take care of people, they won't leave."
- "I'm responsible for everyone's emotional safety."

Even as adults, many Protectors feel uneasy if someone around
them is suffering.

They instinctively reach out, trying to soothe, lighten, solve, repair, or carry the emotional burden.

Their nervous system is trained to brace when others are upset — even when they are not involved.

They feel triggered by tension that has nothing to do with them, because their body remembers when emotional instability meant danger.

THE PROTECTOR IN THE ADULT BODY

Adult Protectors often show up as:

- the listener
- the counselor friend
- the peacekeeper
- the mediator
- the softener
- the caretaker
- the fixer
- the one people confide in
- the one who "holds the room together"

They are the ones others lean on for emotional strength.

They offer support, compassion, and comfort naturally.

But this comes with invisible costs:

- they rarely ask for help
- they feel responsible for the emotional tone of a group
- they worry they've upset someone, even without evidence
- they apologize excessively
- they neglect their own needs
- they feel guilty resting or saying no

- they feel safest when others are calm

For many, the nervous system treats other people's discomfort as a signal of danger — the same way it did in childhood.

WHEN PROTECTION BECOMES A BURDEN

The Protector often carries emotional weight that belongs to others:

- responsibility for someone's feelings
- the need to fix family patterns
- guilt for things they never caused
- caretaking roles that adults should have held
- self-blame for not keeping peace perfectly

This burden is invisible but heavy:

They were not allowed to simply *be* children.
They became little adults emotionally — holding space that was not theirs.

Over time, "protecting" becomes the default way they earn belonging and avoid conflict.

Even love becomes tied to service:

"If I take care of you, you'll stay."
"If I fix this, you'll be happy."
"If I keep peace, I won't be hurt."

The shadow of the Protector is self-erasure.

THE ROOT GIFT OF THE PROTECTOR

The Protector was never meant to be a martyr.

Their instinct to care comes from empathy so strong
it was activated before their voice was fully formed.

When healed, the Protector holds some of the most beautiful
qualities:

- emotional maturity
- deep compassion
- soothing presence
- leadership
- calming energy
- intuitive nurturing
- conflict resolution
- authentic service
- spiritual protection

They are often drawn to healing arts, counseling, Reiki,
teaching, advocacy, or work that elevates others.

The same sensitivity that once took on the pain of others
becomes the ability to recognize needs, set boundaries, and lead
with empathy — without self-sacrifice.

THE TRANSFORMATION OF THE PROTECTOR

Healing does not silence their instinct to help.
It elevates it.

The Protector learns:

- "I can care without carrying."
- "I can support without sacrificing myself."
- "I can offer empathy without absorbing pain."
- "Other people's emotions are not my responsibility."
- "My presence is enough."

They stop operating as a shield
and begin showing up as a guide.

They no longer see themselves as responsible for someone's healing.

Instead, they become a safe companion in someone else's journey.

The adult Protector reclaims balance:

I can hold love and boundaries at the same time.

I can offer support without abandoning myself.

I can care without carrying someone else's weight.

Boundaries do not diminish love —
they refine it.

And when the Protector learns this, their compassion becomes pure rather than heavy.

THE SACRED LESSON OF THE PROTECTOR

This archetype teaches one of the most profound truths in shadow healing:

You are not responsible for the happiness, emotions, or healing of others.

You may influence their journey.
You may support their growth.
You may illuminate their path.
You may hold space with grace.

But you do not need to erase yourself
to make others comfortable.

You do not need to hold peace inside your body
so others feel stable.

You do not need to carry pain
to prove your worth.

You are allowed to breathe.

You are allowed to rest.

You are allowed to exist without fixing anything.

This is the liberation of the Protector:
they stop being the shield
and become the light.

And from that place —
their love is no longer survival.

It is freedom.

THE RETURN TO SELF

The healed Protector turns inward and says:

*"I choose to support others,
but not at the cost of myself."*

They learn that love does not demand sacrifice.
Empathy does not require exhaustion.
Presence does not require silence.
Compassion does not require carrying pain.

They understand that the most powerful way to protect others
is by becoming someone who lives from wholeness.

Because when a Protector heals,
they become a mirror:

"You can heal too."
"You deserve peace too."
"Your emotions are yours, and I trust you to navigate them."

And that trust is a gift.

Instead of shielding others from discomfort,
they empower them to grow.

Instead of absorbing pain,
they hold space.

Instead of fixing,
they listen.

This is the evolution of the Protector:

From emotional guardian in childhood
to compassionate leader in adulthood.

Their shadow becomes their medicine.

Their vigilance becomes intuition.
Their empathy becomes wisdom.
Their responsibility becomes strength.
Their sacrifice becomes service.
Their heaviness becomes light.

And the weight they once carried for the world
turns into the capacity to heal it.

The Disappearing Self

The one who learned that becoming small meant becoming safe.

Some children silence their voice.
Some sharpen their awareness.
Some take responsibility for the emotional landscape around them.

And some do something quieter, more invisible, yet deeply profound:

They disappear.

Not physically —
but emotionally, vibrationally, psychologically, energetically.

The Disappearing Self learned that the safest place to exist was at the edge of attention.

Their presence stayed soft.
Their needs stayed hidden.
Their emotions stayed tucked away.

To survive, they minimized their existence.

HOW THE DISAPPEARING SELF FORMS

The Disappearing Self emerges in childhood environments where:

- unpredictability felt dangerous,
- emotional intensity overwhelmed them,
- attention led to conflict,
- visibility triggered reactions,

- or safety was found in not being noticed.

This child learned that shrinking their presence helped keep equilibrium.

They instinctively reduced their:

- volume
- movement
- needs
- reactions
- visibility
- emotional complexity

They became careful not to disturb peace, not to attract anger, not to awaken scrutiny.

Their internal logic was simple:

"If no one sees me, nothing can hurt me."

This is not weakness.
It is intelligence sculpted by necessity.

THE INTERNAL RULES OF THE DISAPPEARING SELF

From a young age, this archetype carries beliefs such as:

- "It's safer if I stay quiet."
- "The less I need, the better."
- "My emotions are too heavy."
- "I shouldn't burden anyone."
- "If I make myself small, I won't be a target."
- "Attention leads to pain."
- "Invisible is safe."

They may spend childhood:

- fading into the background,
- adapting perfectly to expectations,
- becoming "low maintenance,"
- never asking for help,
- being praised for being "easy," "quiet," or "good."

They appear compliant, gentle, composed.

But this compliance is not personality
—it is survival.

SIGNS OF THE DISAPPEARING SELF IN ADULTHOOD

In adulthood, remnants of this archetype often look like:

- minimizing feelings
- not expressing needs
- avoiding conflict
- withdrawing when overwhelmed
- feeling safer alone
- dissociating under stress
- becoming hyper-independent
- downplaying accomplishments
- giving up space to others
- hiding successes to avoid attention
- feeling uncomfortable being celebrated

They may speak softly, take up minimal physical space, or feel uneasy being the focus of a room.

They are often praised for being:

- calm
- patient
- unproblematic

- agreeable

But beneath that quiet is a deeper truth:

They never learned what it feels like to exist without shrinking.

THE SHADOW PAIN OF DISAPPEARING

This archetype carries a wound that is subtle but profound:

- They were never fully mirrored.
- Their inner world was never fully seen.
- Their emotional landscape went unnoticed.
- Their depth was never reflected back to them.

They learned that their best hope for safety was to become background.

This can lead to:

- feeling unseen in relationships
- believing they do not matter
- losing sense of identity
- struggling to know what they truly want
- difficulty expressing desire
- feeling invisible in groups
- internal loneliness
- difficulty receiving love
- a quiet sense of not existing fully

And yet, even in silence, they hold oceans of depth, empathy, and complexity.

THE SACRED ROOT OF DISAPPEARING

The Disappearing Self did not vanish because they lacked strength.

They vanished because they possessed imagination.

They learned to slip inward, into inner worlds:

- imagination,
- intuition,
- reflection,
- observation,
- sensitivity,
- rich internal perception.

They developed emotional landscapes where they could exist freely
—because their external world did not feel safe enough to hold the fullness of them.

Many of the most creative, intuitive, spiritually gifted adults began as Disappearing Selves.

They developed:

- rich inner dialogue
- powerful empathy
- emotional intelligence
- artistry
- introspection
- spiritual depth

Because the inner world became their sanctuary.

THE EMERGENCE OF SELF

Healing begins gently, gradually, at the pace of safety.

The Disappearing Self does not need to become bold, loud, or forceful.

They simply need permission to exist fully.

It begins with truths like:

- "I am allowed to take up space."
- "My presence matters."
- "My emotions belong."
- "I do not have to hide."
- "Visibility is not danger."
- "I can be seen and still be safe."
- "I am more than my ability to disappear."

The goal is not transformation into someone different — but restoration into someone whole.

Healing means learning:

- to speak even when voice trembles,
- to share even when unsure,
- to occupy space without guilt,
- to let presence be felt,
- to let life see you.

The Disappearing Self does not need to be loud.

They simply need to know that presence is allowed.

THE GIFT OF THE DISAPPEARING SELF

When healed, this archetype becomes profoundly powerful:

- they carry deep compassion
- they understand silence
- they honor vulnerability
- they respect emotional boundaries
- they hold sacred space like few others can

Their quietness transforms from protection
to presence.

Because disappearing children grow into adults who understand
how much courage it takes to exist fully in the world.

They become:

- gentle leaders
- intuitive guides
- compassionate teachers
- spiritually sensitive healers
- storytellers of depth
- artists of emotion
- guardians of empathy

They see people deeply — because they know what it feels like
to be unseen.

THE RETURN TO EXISTENCE

The healed Disappearing Self eventually whispers to their inner
child:

"You don't need to hide anymore.
You are safe.

You are wanted.
You belong here.
I will protect you now."

And slowly, presence returns.

Expression returns.
Identity returns.
Desire returns.
Voice returns.
Belonging returns.

Not in a rush.
Not in a flood.

In soft, steady waves.

The Disappearing Self rises not as someone loud or dominant
—
but as someone deeply whole.

Their re-emergence is quiet, sovereign, grounded.

They show up fully without apologizing for existing.

And the world is better for it.

Because the child who once disappeared
became an adult who understands how to call others back into
themselves.

CHAPTER 12 — Understanding Fear That Wasn't Yours

How to recognize what you absorbed, what you inherited, and what was never yours to carry.

One of the quietest truths in shadow healing is this:

Not all fear inside us comes from our own experiences.

Children are sponges — not only for touch, tone, and words, but for emotional atmosphere.

They do not need explanations to feel danger.
Like animals in nature, they sense emotional climate before they understand the cause.

In this chapter, we explore a foundational principle of shadow work:

Many fears that shape us were not born from our direct experiences —
but from what we absorbed, witnessed, inherited, or interpreted through the body of a child.

This is not imagination.
It is neurobiology, psychology, and transgenerational imprinting.

And learning this truth brings immense compassion to the work of healing.

EMOTIONAL ABSORPTION

Children don't interpret emotion — they absorb it.

Before words form, before logic develops, before reasoning matures, the nervous system scans one thing:

"Is my world safe?"

Children absorb:

- tension,
- silence,
- worry,
- suppressed pain,
- anger that wasn't expressed,
- anxiety that no one admitted,
- grief that stayed unspoken,
- fear that lived behind the eyes of adults.

They absorb posture, tone, breath, and energy.

They may not remember specific events, but the body remembers how the atmosphere felt.

A child can live in a home where nothing "obvious" happened —

and still carry the emotional imprint of threat or instability.

Because the shadow does not form only from what happened…

It also forms from what was *felt*.

FAMILY PROJECTIONS

Children often become containers for emotions adults cannot hold.

When adults are overwhelmed, ashamed, traumatized, or emotionally frozen, their unprocessed inner world often spills outward.

Children may unconsciously take on:

- guilt that wasn't theirs
- blame that wasn't theirs
- responsibility that wasn't theirs
- emotional needs that weren't theirs
- fear that didn't belong to them

A parent might express their anxiety as control.
Their silence as indifference.
Their fear as anger.

The child does not see projection —
they see a reflection of their own worth or danger.

When an adult's internal world is unstable, the child internalizes the message:

*"Something bad is happening...
and I must be the cause, solution, or shield."*

Shadow patterns often begin as attempts to hold the emotional weight that belonged to the adults.

GENERATIONAL FEAR

Sometimes the shadow begins before you were even born.

Neuroscience confirms a powerful truth:

Fear, stress, and trauma markers can pass through generational lines

through DNA expression, nervous system programming, and family behavior patterns.

Meaning:

What your body learned to fear might not have begun with you.

History, culture, religion, migration, poverty, war, and abuse all leave emotional fingerprints on families — even when never spoken aloud.

You may carry fragments of:

- your mother's unhealed wounds
- your father's shame
- your grandmother's suppressed terror
- your ancestors' survival instincts
- generational secrets
- inherited silence

Families who lived under emotional suppression often raise children hypersensitive to danger.
Families who survived betrayal raise children cautious of vulnerability.
Families who endured shame raise children terrified of being seen.

You may have been born into a story that shaped your emotional DNA before your story even began.

WHAT YOU "PICKED UP" VS WHAT YOU LIVED

Many adults judge themselves for fears they cannot logically justify:

- fear of anger
- fear of abandonment
- fear of punishment
- fear of conflict
- fear of being seen
- fear of being wrong
- fear of wanting too much
- fear of taking up space

But the body may be responding to:

- atmospheres you lived in,
- emotions you absorbed,
- beliefs passed down,
- stories spoken in fragments,
- moments you witnessed but cannot fully recall,
- or feelings no one explained out loud.

For many people, the nervous system isn't reacting to an event…

It's reacting to *interpretation.*

To the energetic climate.

To the emotional weight that surrounded them as children.

A child who sees adults overwhelmed, frightened, or unstable develops fear —
even if the fear was never directed at them personally.

Because children do not separate their experience from the emotional weather around them.

They *become* it.

And that emotional imprint travels into adulthood as shadow.

THE COMPASSION IN THIS TRUTH

Understanding that some fears were absorbed, inherited, or projected onto you changes everything.

It shifts healing from judgment to tenderness.

Instead of:

"Why am I like this?"
"What's wrong with me?"
"Why can't I just move on?"

We begin to ask:

"What emotion did my child-self absorb that didn't belong to me?"
"What fear am I carrying for someone who couldn't hold it themselves?"
"What belief did I mistake as truth simply because no one named the real cause?"

The moment we question the origin of fear,
we loosen its power.

We begin to see that what lives in us might be:

- echoes
- imprints
- inherited shadows
- emotional memories
- nervous system adaptations

Not personal flaws.

RELEASING INHERITED EMOTIONS

Healing fear that wasn't ours requires gentle recognition:

1. **Name what you absorbed.**
    Not as blame —
    but as clarity.
    - o "I carried my mother's anxiety without knowing."
    - o "I absorbed the fear of anger because I sensed it in the home."
    - o "I inherited silence because generations before me survived by staying quiet."
2. **Separate story from identity.**
    - o "This fear was present in my childhood, but it is not who I am now."
3. **Return responsibility.**
    Quietly and compassionately:
    - o "This emotion is not mine to carry anymore."
4. **Allow the nervous system to update.**
    When the adult self meets the child's belief with truth, the body learns safety.
5. **Cultivate compassion for the ones who came before.**
    Most adults did not project fear intentionally —
    they simply didn't know how to hold their own wounds.

Releasing inherited fear is not rejection of family, history, or experience.

It is liberation.

It is saying:

"What happened around me shaped me,
but it does not define who I am becoming."

THE GENTLE PROMISE OF THIS WORK

When you realize that part of your shadow was formed from
fear that wasn't yours...

healing becomes less like digging through the past
and more like returning to truth:

- You were sensitive enough to feel emotional landscapes.
- You were perceptive enough to absorb what others hid.
- You were intuitive enough to notice what adults could
  not name.
- You were empathic enough to carry what was too heavy
  for those around you.

And now,
you are strong enough to release it.

This is not detachment.
It is freedom.

The shadow begins to heal when you lovingly hand back the
emotional weight that was never meant to rest on your
shoulders.

The child within you did not misinterpret.

They simply absorbed what they could not yet explain.

Today,
you have language.

You have wisdom.
You have awareness.
You have safety.
You have compassion.

And with those, you can lay down what was not yours.

So you can walk forward lighter,
clearer,
and more fully yourself.

CHAPTER 13 — Rewriting the Story of the Inner Child

Healing begins when the adult self offers the child the truth they never received.

By the time we reach this stage of shadow healing, something profound has already happened:

You are no longer looking at your childhood through the eyes of the child who lived it.

You are seeing it as the adult who survived it.

This shift is where transformation begins.

Because children do not have context, neuroscience, perspective, or emotional language.
They do not understand:

- addiction,
- trauma,
- stress patterns,
- mental illness,
- generational wounds,
- or survival responses.

They only understand *"This feels scary"* or *"This feels safe."*

Shadow work helps us go back — not to relive the past, but to reinterpret it.

To correct what the child believed.
To offer compassion where fear once lived.
To give safety where silence once ruled.

This is rewriting the story of the inner child.

CORRECTING MISINTERPRETATIONS

The child's conclusions were logical — but incomplete.

When a child experiences emotional instability, they reach for meaning.
Because meaning creates the illusion of control.

Their logic is simple and self-directed:

- "If I caused this, I can prevent it."
- "If I'm quiet, nothing bad happens."
- "If I take care of everyone, they won't get upset."
- "If I disappear, I won't be hurt."

These interpretations are not childish mistakes.
They are survival strategies.

But now — as adults — we carry beliefs based on feelings we once couldn't name.

Healing begins by gently offering the child within us a new interpretation — one based on truth, not fear.

Examples of re-interpretation:

- "My parent's anger was about their pain, not my worth."
- "I stayed quiet because it helped me feel safe, not because my voice is unimportant."
- "I learned to watch closely because the environment was unpredictable, not because danger is everywhere."
- "I cared for others because I loved deeply, not because I was responsible for their emotions."

Reframing removes blame from the child and returns accountability to the adults, circumstances, and systems that shaped the atmosphere.

It brings compassion to a story that was never meant to be carried alone.

RE-PARENTING WITH COMPASSION

The adult self becomes the parent the child needed.

Re-parenting is not about altering the past —
it's about meeting the emotional wounds with present-day care.

It sounds like this:

- "You did nothing wrong."
- "Your emotions matter."
- "You were not responsible for anyone's pain."
- "You deserved protection, presence, and tenderness."
- "I believe you."
- "I am here for you now."

Re-parenting replaces fear with safety, shame with dignity, and confusion with clarity.

It allows the adult self to become:

- the protector,
- the listener,
- the validator,
- the comforter,
- the emotional anchor

the child never had.

Re-parenting doesn't force bravery or demand strength.
It offers warmth, patience, and presence.

It responds to the wounded child with kindness instead of criticism.

CREATING EMOTIONAL SAFETY INSIDE

Your nervous system responds to inner truth more powerfully than outer reassurance.

For many people, the deepest pain of childhood was not the event —
but the emotional isolation around it.

Feeling unsafe without a witness.
Feeling frightened without comfort.
Feeling confused without validation.

That is why emotional safety today matters so profoundly.

Emotional safety sounds like:

- "I'm allowed to feel this."
- "I don't have to rush my healing."
- "I can soothe myself instead of abandoning myself."
- "I can sit with my emotions instead of silencing them."

Internal safety is when you stop treating your feelings as threats.

When your nervous system learns:

"Feeling is not danger.
Expression is not danger.
Remembering is not danger.
Existing is not danger."

It begins to relax.

And relaxation is the doorway to integration.

INTEGRATING THE LOST SELF

Your inner child does not need to "heal" — they need to come home.

Many people think shadow work means fixing the child inside them.

But the child was never broken.

They were frightened, intuitive, and doing the best they could with limited resources.

Integration is not altering the child —
it is retrieving them from the places they hid.

It is welcoming back the parts that froze, watched, protected, or disappeared.

The adult self becomes the safe place where the child can finally:

- speak,
- feel,
- rest,
- breathe,
- be seen,
- be validated.

Integration looks like:

- noticing when your inner child is triggered
- pausing rather than reacting
- offering comfort instead of criticism
- listening to the fear without believing it
- inviting that child to stand beside you, not beneath you

Because the child in you is not a wound.

They are a witness.
A protector.
A survivor.
A holder of intuition.
A keeper of your earliest truth.

The goal is not to "erase" them.

It is to give them space in your heart as part of your wholeness.

To say:

"Thank you for protecting me.
You don't have to carry this alone anymore."

And when those lost parts return,
something extraordinary happens:

- confidence rises,
- voice strengthens,
- intuition awakens,
- identity clarifies,
- self-trust deepens.

Because you are no longer fragmented between past and present.

You become one person instead of two.

THE HEART OF REWRITING THE STORY

Rewriting the inner child's story does not change what happened.
It changes what it *meant*.

You no longer see yourself as damaged, invisible, responsible, weak, or afraid.

You see yourself as:

- adaptive,
- intuitive,
- empathetic,
- resilient,
- and capable of extraordinary love.

Your childhood becomes not a wound that defines you,
but a landscape that shaped your insight.

A story that gave birth to your purpose.

Shadow work reveals that the deepest pain of childhood
becomes the greatest wisdom of adulthood.

And when you rewrite the story with compassion,
you make room for the child within you to step into the light of
your becoming.

Because they were never the shadow.

They were the beginning of your light.

SECTION IV — THE REIKI SHADOW INTEGRATION METHOD

CHAPTER 14 — Why Energy Work Matters in Shadow Healing

Because shadow is not only psychological — it is energetic.

Shadow work is often spoken about through emotion, memory, and mindset.
But those who have walked the healing path deeply know something more:

Shadow is not just a story in the mind.

It is a pattern in the nervous system.
A resonance in the aura.
A constriction in the chakras.
A frequency held in the tissues and field.

This is why energy work — especially modalities like Reiki — becomes profoundly important.

It does not erase the past.
It clears the energetic imprint of how the body carried it.

SHADOW ENERGY IN THE AURA

The auric field stores what consciousness tried to forget.

When emotional shock, fear, overwhelm, shame, or confusion occurs, the body tries to understand it.

If the mind cannot — because the experience was too young, too fast, too disorienting, or too unsafe — the memory moves into the field.

The aura records:

- tone
- sensation
- threat
- emotional climate
- tension in the home
- the moment safety was questioned

Even when the event is forgotten, the energetic imprint remains.

This can show up as:

- heaviness around the solar plexus
- pressure across the chest
- a dense field around the heart
- tightness behind the shoulders
- a porous boundary layer
- a foggy feeling around the head
- an unsettled field at the root

The aura holds what the child could not process with language.

And energy healing brings these imprints into light — softly, safely, gradually — in a way that talk alone cannot.

WHERE FEAR SITS IN THE CHAKRAS

Each chakra reveals how the body translated emotional threat.

Fear does not distribute randomly.
It follows energetic pathways that reflect survival needs, emotional development, and intuitive responses.

Here are common shadow imprints:

ROOT CHAKRA — Safety

Fear stored here comes from instability, unpredictability, or physical threat.
It manifests as hypervigilance, scarcity beliefs, or a background feeling of "something could go wrong."

SACRAL CHAKRA — Emotion & Innocence

Imprints here relate to shame, emotional suppression, or unsafe relationships.
It influences vulnerability and emotional intimacy.

SOLAR PLEXUS — Power & Identity

Shadow here shows up as guilt, self-blame, perfectionism, or the feeling of needing to stay "small" to remain safe.

HEART CHAKRA — Connection

Here lie imprints of abandonment, betrayal, emotional freezing, and the belief that love is conditional or dangerous.

THROAT CHAKRA — Expression

Silence, swallowing words, fear of speaking truth, or childhood environments where honesty felt unsafe.

THIRD EYE — Perception

Overactive intuition born from survival-based observation: "I must watch closely or I won't be safe."

CROWN CHAKRA — Belonging to Source

When childhood fear damages spiritual trust, people may unconsciously believe they are alone, unsupported, or unworthy of protection.

As shadow softens through energy work, these chakras begin to release:

- constriction,
- stored memory,
- emotional residue,
- instinctive defense patterns.

The result?

A nervous system that no longer expects threat.

A field that begins to breathe again.

THE FREEZE IMPRINT

When the body decides stillness is survival.

Many children respond to fear not with fight or flight — but freeze.

Freeze is the body's last defense when danger feels:

- unpredictable,
- too large,
- too intimate,
- too complex,

- or too confusing to understand.

Freeze imprints are some of the most common energetic scars carried into adulthood.

They may look like:

- chronic tension
- numb emotional response
- dissociation
- distrust of joy
- difficulty feeling present
- shutting down when overwhelmed
- or struggle to relax when everything is actually safe

This imprint isn't weakness.

It's the body honoring the best survival choice it had at the time.

Energy work helps melt the freeze response from the field by:

- increasing circulation to the nervous system pathways
- expanding contraction patterns in the aura
- calming the instinctive fight/flight signals
- releasing cellular-level emotional codes
- restoring the body's access to sensation and presence

When the freeze imprint dissolves, many people are amazed by how much aliveness returns.

They feel:

- more present in their body
- safer in expression
- connected to their desires
- aware of their intuition
- and emotionally fluid again

AURA DISTORTION AND REPAIR

Shadow distortions are not damage — they are defense.

In shadow states, the aura may:

- contract tightly at the solar plexus
- fragment outward in the heart field
- harden at the root
- fog over at the crown
- build density around the throat
- thin at the boundaries
- form "gaps" where energy drained in childhood

These distortions once served a purpose:

- shielding
- shrinking
- protection
- insulation
- emotional numbness

But in adulthood, they create limitation:

- fear of visibility
- hypervigilance
- emotional distance
- boundary confusion
- low vitality
- persistent self-doubt
- difficulty trusting connection

Reiki softens these distortions gently.

Not by force —
but by raising frequency.

When frequency rises, emotional residue loosens and begins to clear:

- shame
- confusion
- inherited beliefs
- childhood fears
- emotional memories
- subconscious tensions

The aura reorganizes itself.

It becomes clearer, more coherent, and more expansive.

The person regains a sense of:

- safety,
- groundedness,
- self-trust,
- personal power,
- emotional resilience,
- and ease in their own energy.

This is the heart of why energy work matters in shadow healing:

It rewrites the emotional blueprint that the shadow lived inside.

THE BRIDGE BETWEEN ENERGY AND PSYCHOLOGY

Talk therapy gives language, insight, and perspective.
Energy work restores:

- safety,
- presence,
- coherence,
- and embodiment.

Together, they form the wholeness of shadow healing.

Because shadow is emotional, psychological, spiritual, nervous-system based, and energetic all at once.

And for many people, the deepest transformation happens not when they understand their past —

but when the body finally releases what it has carried for decades.

Reiki brings the shadow out of hiding
not through pain,
but through peace.

Shadow dissolves not through force,
but through frequency.

And the child who once froze, hid, protected, or watched finally feels safe enough to breathe again.

CHAPTER 15 — Dissolving the Past at the Root

Releasing energetic cords, reclaiming your identity, and calling your soul back into fullness.

Shadow work is not complete when you understand the past.

It is complete when the past loosens its hold on your energy, beliefs, identity, and sense of self.

This chapter explores the deepest layer of shadow release:

Dissolving the root imprint.

Not the memory.
Not the history.
Not the story.

But the *energetic cord* that keeps the nervous system bound to an emotional truth that is no longer real.

To dissolve shadow at the root is to give the inner child permission to step out of the past and into safety — fully, freely, completely.

YOUR METHOD OF CORD DISSOLUTION

Energetic cords form where emotional imprint once mattered for survival.

An energetic cord is not a supernatural tether.
It is the residue of identity.

It forms where the child made meaning in order to survive:

- a belief,
- a fear,
- an emotional conclusion,
- a protective instinct,
- a pattern of watching, hiding, pleasing, or shrinking.

The cord exists only where the child's nervous system said:

"I must hold onto this to stay safe."

Cord dissolution is not cutting away the past.

It is releasing the emotional contract that formed there.

It affirms:

- "This belief is no longer true."
- "This fear no longer protects me."
- "This identity no longer belongs to me."

Your method of cord dissolution can be done through Reiki, intention, visualization, breath, light, or touch.

The key isn't technique —
it's clarity:

You release the meaning, not the memory.
You dissolve the imprint, not the story.

Cord dissolution leaves the past intact —
but removes its power over the present.

REMOVING ENERGETIC RESIDUE

The emotional "after-scent" of the past.

Even after the cord dissolves, energetic residue may linger.

Residue is:

- tense patterns
- thought habits
- triggers
- reflexive fear
- flinching around vulnerability
- bracing during conflict
- bursts of shame with no clear source

Residue is not shadow.

It is muscle memory.

It unwinds gradually through:

- Reiki
- breathwork
- grounding
- emotional validation
- chakra balancing
- compassionate witnessing
- time spent in safety

Think of it as the nervous system exhaling after decades of holding its breath.

Residue is a sign the cord has loosened,
and the body is recalibrating.

Not everything vanishes at once —
it dissolves layer by layer,
after the root meaning has been released.

STRENGTHENING THE NEW IDENTITY

Once the old belief dissolves, the inner self needs a replacement truth.

People often ask,
"Once I release the old pattern, what goes in its place?"

The answer is:
Your real identity.

Identity is the part that trauma cannot touch.

Who you were always meant to be —
beneath fear, silence, hyper-awareness, or self-erasure.

After cord dissolution, the adult self must anchor new truths:

- "I can take up space."
- "I am safe to feel."
- "I deserve tenderness."
- "My voice matters."
- "I trust myself."
- "I belong here."
- "I am whole."

This becomes the new energetic blueprint.

And as identity strengthens,
the shadow no longer needs to protect you.

Because protection is no longer required.

You are living from truth instead of survival.

SOUL RECLAMATION

The moment when the child returns home to the self.

Shadow healing does not end with release.

It ends with return.

With the moment the inner child
walks back into the heart of the adult self
and becomes part of their wholeness again.

Soul reclamation is when you:

- recognize your sensitivity as a gift
- see your vigilance as intuition
- honor your compassion
- allow your presence to be felt
- speak without shrinking
- love without fear
- exist without apology

It is the moment when the child who hid, froze, watched, or carried too much
is no longer separate from you...

but united.

Their wisdom, instinct, imagination, intuition, and empathy become the foundation of who you are.

Not brokenness.

Wholeness.

Not loss.

Integration.

Not a missing piece.

A restored one.

Soul reclamation is the final phase of shadow healing:

When you stand rooted and calm,
knowing the past shaped you,
but no longer defines you.

The cord dissolves.

The residue clears.

The identity settles.

And the soul that once fractured for safety
returns home to itself.

Fully.

Freely.

Completely.

SECTION V — BECOMING THE LIGHT

CHAPTER 16 — Becoming the Cycle-Breaker

Ending the inheritance of pain, choosing truth over silence, and becoming the adult your childhood needed.

To heal your shadow is a personal act.
To break the cycle is a generational one.

Cycle-breaking is what happens when you no longer continue the patterns that came before you — even if you inherited the trauma, the fear, or the beliefs.

It is the moment where the past meets a wall and stops, because someone chose differently.

That someone is you.

You are the pivot point.
The interruption.
The first breath of a new lineage.

And nothing proves this more powerfully than the four markers of a true cycle-breaker: healthy boundaries, the end of inherited silence, identity by choice rather than imprint, and becoming the adult you once needed.

HEALTHY BOUNDARIES

The cycle ends where self-betrayal ends.

People who grew up in emotional instability rarely learned healthy boundaries:

- you didn't get to voice needs
- "no" felt dangerous
- feelings were swallowed
- discomfort was avoided
- the safest thing was peacekeeping

Boundaries felt like conflict.
Conflict felt like threat.

So one of the clearest signs of becoming a cycle-breaker is this shift:

You no longer abandon yourself to keep the peace.

Healthy boundaries aren't walls — they are clarity.

They sound like:

- "That doesn't feel right for me."
- "I need space."
- "I'm not responsible for your emotions."
- "I love you, but I will not participate in this dynamic."
- "My needs matter, too."

A boundary is not rejection —
it is self-respect.

When you choose truth instead of compliance,
your nervous system learns that you can be safe and self-honoring at the same time.

And that is the internal moment when the chain breaks.

THE END OF SILENCE

Silence was a survival strategy — not your nature.

For those with shadow-imprints, silence once meant:

- safety
- invisibility
- compliance
- protection

Words were dangerous.
Truth felt explosive.
Sound could wake the person you feared.

Breaking the cycle does not require public storytelling —
it requires that you no longer stay silent where truth is needed.

It is the moment "quiet" stops being instinct
and becomes a choice.

You recognize:

- speaking clarity is not betrayal
- expressing needs is not selfish
- naming harm is not disloyal
- telling the truth is not dangerous

The cycle breaks when:

- you speak up for your child
- you call out abuse
- you choose honesty over appeasement
- you refuse to gaslight yourself
- you stop protecting the one who caused pain

- you tell your own story on your own terms

Silence becomes unnecessary
because safety is no longer dependent on it.

When the voice returns,
the lineage changes.

CHOOSING WHO YOU ARE

Instead of living as who fear trained you to be.

Trauma creates identities unconsciously:

- The quiet one
- The watcher
- The caretaker
- The invisible self

They formed to protect the child.

But cycle-breaking begins when identity becomes intentional
rather than inherited.

When you choose:

- "I am confident."
- "I am worthy."
- "I am safe being visible."
- "I can take up space."
- "I speak when something matters."
- "I trust my instincts."
- "I do not try to earn safety by shrinking."

Identity becomes freedom,
not defense.

And this shift doesn't just alter your life —

It alters the emotional DNA of everyone who comes after you:

Children raised by a healed parent learn:

- boundaries,
- communication,
- emotional literacy,
- safe self-expression,
- inner worth.

The cycle breaks one decision at a time
until those decisions become truth.

BECOMING THE ADULT YOU NEEDED

The final transformation of shadow healing.

Every cycle-breaker eventually discovers this truth:

You cannot rewrite the past.
But you can become the person who would have made it gentle.

That is the real triumph.

Cycle-breakers become:

- the protector they did not have
- the voice they needed spoken over them
- the safety that was missing
- the softness that would have changed everything
- the advocate they deserved

They parent differently.
They speak differently.
They love differently.

They walk through the world with consciousness that was forged from their own survival.

They no longer shame their sensitivity
but honor it as the compass that guided them.

They do not punish vulnerability
but protect it.

They do not silence truth
but defend it gently and fiercely.

They live in alignment with a very simple vow:

"The pain stops here."

Not because the past didn't happen.
Not because the wound vanished.
Not because memory is erased.

But because you learned:

- how to tell the truth,
- how to set boundaries,
- how to listen to your intuition,
- how to honor your inner child,
- how to live from compassion rather than fear.

You are the first generation of healedness —
and those who come after you will never know what you carried.

Because you made a choice.

Cycle-breakers are not louder, braver, or stronger than others.

They are simply the ones who decided that their story would not continue through another heartbeat, another home, another child, another lifetime.

Instead, you created something new:

Safety.
Awareness.
Empowerment.
Love that doesn't harm.
Honesty without punishment.
Generations free of fear.

You became the adult your inner child hoped existed somewhere.

And you became the reason your lineage now heals.

CHAPTER 17 — Writing a New Future

Identity shifts, self-worth, emotional sovereignty, and choosing to live from light instead of reaction.

Shadow work is about looking back long enough to understand, release, and reclaim.

But the purpose of healing is not to stay in the past.

It is to step forward.

When the root cords dissolve, the inner child integrates, and old beliefs fall away, something subtle begins to happen:

You are no longer living *from* the past —
you are living *toward* something new.

You stop reacting to what shaped you
and start creating what calls you.

This is the moment shadow work becomes light work.

It is the threshold between who survival required you to be
and who your soul is now free to become.

IDENTITY SHIFTS

You are no longer the person built by fear.

Most people arrive at shadow work with an identity structured by:

- caution
- emotional suppression
- guilt
- shame
- shrinking
- over-responsibility
- watching others more than themselves

They use traits shaped by past fear to navigate present life.

But when the shadow dissolves at the root, identity begins to re-form — not around protection, but around truth.

Signs of identity shifting:

- you speak without rehearsing
- you no longer shrink to soften others
- you take up space without apology
- your tone becomes calmer and more grounded
- your body feels present
- you no longer try to "earn" safety
- your decisions come from intuition, not fear

You are not becoming someone different.

You are becoming who you would have been
if fear had never been there.

Identity ceases to be a response to danger
and becomes an expression of authenticity.

SELF-WORTH

You stop negotiating with your own value.

Shadow-trained children often learned toxic self-concepts:

- "I'm only safe if I'm quiet."
- "I have to be perfect."
- "I shouldn't need anything."
- "Other people matter more than me."

Self-worth becomes conditional, fragile, and externally measured.

But healing realigns self-worth from the inside:

- you no longer need validation to feel real
- you no longer tie your value to usefulness
- you no longer justify your existence
- you stop apologizing for having emotions
- you stop shrinking to make others comfortable
- you stop tolerating disrespect

Self-worth becomes intrinsic, not negotiated.

It sounds like:

"I matter because I exist."
"I am worthy of tenderness and respect."
"I deserve emotional safety and truth."
"I am allowed to be seen, heard, and valued."

When self-worth roots deeply, the entire nervous system shifts.

You speak differently.
You walk differently.

You choose differently.
You love differently.
You breathe differently.

You begin living as someone who knows they are enough.

And life rises to meet that belief.

EMOTIONAL SOVEREIGNTY

Your feelings belong to you — and you are not ruled by them.

In shadow-imprinted living, emotions feel dangerous:

- suppressed
- ignored
- minimized
- hidden
- feared

Emotional sovereignty is the opposite.

It is a state where feelings are heard, understood, and allowed — without flooding the mind or hijacking the body.

You learn:

- "My anger is information, not a threat."
- "My sadness is a signal, not a weakness."
- "My fear needs compassion, not silence."
- "My joy is safe, not fragile."

Emotion no longer drags you backward.

It moves you forward.

You respond rather than react.
You express rather than implode.
You listen to your body rather than fight it.

Emotional sovereignty means:

- triggers invite reflection
- discomfort becomes a teacher
- boundaries come with calm clarity
- relationships align with authenticity
- empathy no longer leads to self-sacrifice
- you do not carry responsibility that isn't yours

You become emotionally anchored —
present, rooted, aware, and awake.

This is the most profound sign that the shadow has been integrated rather than feared:

Your emotions no longer silence you —
they guide you.

LIVING IN LIGHT, NOT REACTION

The past stops steering the future.

When shadow patterns dissolve,
you stop living in reaction to what you survived.

Your choices are no longer shaped by:

- fear
- guilt
- hypervigilance
- inherited beliefs
- old power dynamics

Instead, your life becomes guided by:

- joy
- intuition
- purpose
- truth
- creativity
- spiritual connection
- compassion toward self and others

You begin living from light —
the inner knowing that you are safe, sovereign, and whole.

Living in light looks like:

- choosing relationships that feel gentle
- letting go of those who drain or diminish you
- trusting your voice without rehearsing your tone
- telling the truth without trembling
- walking away from what hurts
- welcoming what nourishes
- loving without self-erasure
- creating instead of coping
- allowing softness without fear

Your nervous system rewrites its primary directive:

"I must hide to survive"
becomes
"I am safe to be fully myself."

And future actions flow from safety, not fear.

THE NEW FUTURE

The shadow becomes wisdom, not identity.

Healing does not erase what happened.
It transforms its meaning.

The past becomes:

- lesson,
- clarity,
- intuition,
- discernment,
- compassion,
- strength,
- depth.

Your story becomes a source of light rather than a weight.

You carry empathy that can detect pain in others.
You carry understanding that allows you to hold space without judgment.
You carry intuition that reads situations with clarity.
You carry strength that exists without hardness.

And the future is no longer something to brace for.

It is something you shape.

The new future sounds like:

"I choose."
"I trust."
"I grow."
"I give myself what I once lacked."

"I build what I was never given."
"I rise without apology."

Your identity, self-worth, voice, heart, boundaries, intuition, and emotions finally belong to you.

Not to the past.

Not to the shadow.

Not to fear.

To you.

And from that place, you begin living not as the child who survived —
but as the adult who creates.

You write your future now.

One truth at a time.
One choice at a time.
One breath at a time.

In light.
In freedom.
In fullness.
In wholeness.

CHAPTER 18 — The Gifts Your Shadows Gave You

Intuition, Empathy, Discernment, Purpose, and Spiritual Depth

When people think of shadow work, they focus on wounds.

But what they rarely recognize is that many of the traits they love most about themselves —
the wisdom, awareness, compassion, intuition —
were formed in the very same moments they learned to survive.

The shadow is shaped by pain, yes.

But the gifts forged in that darkness are powerful.

They are the treasures mined in the places the light didn't reach.

This chapter is the acknowledgment that you are not only healing from your past —
you are also honoring what it gave you.

Not the harm.
Not the trauma.
But the skills, instincts, depth, and sensitivity that only emerge through emotional fire.

Here are five gifts born from the shadow.

INTUITION

Your nervous system learned to see what others overlooked.

Children who grow up in volatility learn to read a room before they enter it:

- tone of voice
- body language
- subtle changes in energy
- emotional shifts
- danger signals
- unspoken tension

This hyper-awareness was once survival.

But when healed,
it becomes extraordinary intuition.

It becomes the ability to:

- sense truth
- understand people deeply
- predict emotional movement
- read behind words
- detect dishonesty
- feel energetic imbalance
- perceive spiritual nuance

Where others walk through life blind to patterns, you feel them.

This is intuition sharpened by necessity,
but transformed by healing into wisdom.

It becomes less about bracing for threat,
and more about perceiving reality clearly.

The shadow gave you refined perception.
The healing gives you trust in it.

EMPATHY

You feel deeply because you learned what pain feels like.

Those who have suffered rarely become indifferent.

Instead, they develop empathy that is:

- profound
- sincere
- compassionate
- nonjudgmental
- emotionally intelligent

You understand fear because you've felt it.
You hold space easily because you needed it once.
You listen differently because you know silence intimately.

Your empathy is not weakness — it is sacred capacity.

It lets you:

- comfort the hurting
- offer safety without words
- recognize unspoken stories
- support others without demand
- forgive without forgetting
- understand complexity

Empathy from shadow survivors is not naïve.

It is fierce.

It knows what harm can do —
and chooses gentleness anyway.

This gift becomes your contribution to the world:
you treat others with the softness you once needed most.

DISCERNMENT

You learned early that not everyone is safe — and that wisdom became spiritual intelligence.

When you grow up in instability,
you learn quickly:

- who feels safe
- what feels off
- when a story doesn't align
- when energy shifts
- who hides secrets
- when words contradict behavior

Discernment is intuition with clarity.

It is the ability to see truth without explanation.

In adulthood, it becomes:

- better boundaries
- selective relationships
- honest self-reflection
- courage to walk away
- protection without paranoia
- spiritual intelligence

Discernment is the shadow's refinement.

It is how darkness becomes vision.

PURPOSE

Your pain gave you a direction — a reason to heal, to serve, to rise.

People who have survived emotional wounds rarely wander aimlessly.

They are driven.

They want to understand:

- themselves,
- humanity,
- spirit,
- suffering,
- healing,
- transformation.

Shadow-born purpose sounds like:

- "I want to help others not feel alone."
- "I want to offer the safety I never had."
- "I want to create better than what I experienced."
- "I feel called to guide, teach, or heal."
- "I want to build a life rooted in truth."

This is why so many trauma survivors are teachers, healers, guides, therapists, mentors, and spiritual practitioners.

Pain strips away distraction.
Shadow makes clarity urgent.

Purpose becomes the natural consequence of awakening.

The shadow gave you direction —
healing gives you the ability to walk it fully.

SPIRITUAL DEPTH

Those who have walked in darkness do not fear their inner world — they understand it.

When someone has survived:

- fear,
- shame,
- betrayal,
- powerlessness,
- silence,
- loneliness,

they gain a unique spiritual depth.

They know the landscape of the soul.

They have visited the inner cave —
sat with the dark
and faced their own reflection.

This produces:

- humility
- compassion
- wisdom
- spiritual discernment
- reverence for life
- inner stillness
- connection with the unseen
- emotional intelligence
- a deeper relationship with truth

Shadow survivors often become spiritual seekers because the ordinary world never answered the questions they were forced to ask:

- What makes us who we are?
- How does the soul heal?
- What is truth?
- What is love?
- Why do people harm?
- What exists beyond the visible?

This depth becomes a path.

It opens the door to healing arts,
intuitive awareness,
Reiki,
energy medicine,
and profound inner transformation.

The shadow did not dim your light.
It prepared you to hold it.

THE ALCHEMY OF THE SHADOW

When the shadow heals,
the wound becomes wisdom,
the fear becomes intuition,
the silence becomes clarity,
and the pain becomes purpose.

You do not glorify what happened —
you honor what it forged.

Your past did not define your worth —
it awakened it.

Your shadow did not steal your spirit —
it carved out the space where your spirit now sits.

The gifts it gave you are not scars.

They are sacred intelligence.

They are proof that:

- you survived,
- you adapted,
- you learned,
- you rose,
- you transformed,
- you became more, not less.

And now, as you step forward,
you carry the very things that once protected you —
but they are no longer armor.

They are light.

CHAPTER 19 — A Letter to the Child You Once Were

Final Integration, Closure, and Wholeness

Close your eyes for a moment
and imagine the small version of you —

the one who watched,
the one who stayed quiet,
the one who learned to read danger in silence,
the one who carried weight too heavy for small hands.

See them as they were.

Tiny.
Tender.
Hopeful.
Confused.
Brilliant.
Sensitive.
Trying so hard to make sense of a world so much bigger than them.

This chapter is a letter
to that child.

Not as a stranger —
but as the adult they grew into.

The one who survived.
The one who healed.
The one who finally knows the truth.

This letter is final integration.

It is closure.

It is the moment the child and the adult
become one, without separation.

A LETTER TO THE ONE WHO SURVIVED

Dear Little One,

I see you.

I know you held your breath more than you spoke.
I know you learned silence to stay safe.
I know you watched everything,
your body alert long before you had words for why.

You took responsibility that never belonged to you.
You carried guilt that wasn't yours.
You worried about the feelings of people
who should have been worrying about you.

You made yourself small,
not because you were weak,
but because you were wise.

You did what you needed to survive.

And I want you to know this:

You did nothing wrong.

The fear was real.
The confusion was real.
The instinct to disappear was real.

Everything you did
made sense for who you were
and where you were.

You were not fragile —
you were incredibly intelligent.

You shaped yourself around danger.
You adapted to emotional instability.
You learned to sense what could not be said out loud.

And every one of those instincts
became a gift in my life.

I survived because of you.

I learned to trust intuition because of you.
I learned empathy because of you.
I learned discernment because of you.
I learned compassion because of you.
I developed purpose because of you.
I found spiritual depth because of you.

You were never the problem.

You were the answer.

The one who stayed alert
so I could grow up safe.

The one who read energy
so I could navigate wisely.

The one who remained quiet
so I could learn the strength of my own voice later.

You protected me
when no one else knew how.

There is no part of you I reject.
There is no memory of you I judge.
There is no version of you I wish away.

You are welcome here.

All of you.

The scared child.
The silent child.
The intuitive child.
The one who froze.
The one who hid.
The one who waited.
The one who couldn't understand
but tried anyway.

You did your best.
And your best was extraordinary.

You are safe now.

I am here.
I am grown.
I know the difference between fear and truth.
I know when to stay, and when to walk away.
I know how to protect us.
I know how to listen, to speak, to love, to stand tall.

You do not need to keep watch anymore.
You do not need to be silent anymore.
You do not need to shrink.
You do not need to stay small.
You do not need to carry what was never yours.

I promise you:

No one will hurt us again.
I will keep us safe.
I will choose people worthy of our heart.
I will listen when we feel uncertain.
I will hold space for every emotion,
even the ones we once feared.

You can rest now.

You can play.
You can breathe.
You can be seen.
You can laugh.
You can feel.
You can grow.
You can trust.

Because I am finally here —
awake, aware, healed, whole.

You are not a memory I carry.
You are the root of who I became:

Wise.
Strong.
Compassionate.
Intuitive.
Boundaried.

Empowered.
Whole.

Thank you for surviving.

Thank you for holding the story
until I was ready to tell it.

Thank you for protecting the softness
that I now carry proudly.

I love you.
I see you.
I choose you.
I honor you.
I am you.

And we are finally safe.

Welcome home.

— Your Future Self

THE MOMENT OF FINAL INTEGRATION

Your story does not end with the wound.

It ends with this wholeness —
the child and adult reunited.

All shadow work leads here:

to the return.

Where the inner child is no longer a memory held at arm's
length,
but a living presence inside the heart,
embraced with tenderness,
protected with boundaries,
guided by truth,
and honored as sacred.

Integration is not forgetting.
Integration is *belonging.*

It is when you no longer fear the past
because it no longer owns your nervous system.

It is when the inner child is not a ghost,
but a companion.

It is when the story no longer hurts,
but informs.

It is when you walk through the world not as someone
wounded,
but as someone expanded.

You do not become whole by erasing the shadow.

You become whole by holding every part of yourself
with compassion and truth.

CLOSURE

Closure is not a doorway that locks behind you.

It is a gentle breath.

It is the moment the body recognizes:
"We are safe now."

The memories remain,
but without the ache.

The past exists,
but without ownership.

You walk with clarity,
with tenderness,
with truth,
and with the freedom to write every next moment
from light instead of fear.

WHOLENESS

Wholeness is not perfection.

It is integration.

It is becoming the adult who looks at the child inside and says:

"I will love you the way you always deserved."

Wholeness is when your sensitivity becomes wisdom,
your pain becomes purpose,
your fear becomes intuition,
your vigilance becomes awareness,
and your story becomes strength.

This is not an ending.

It is the beginning of a life rooted in truth, compassion, and
sovereignty.

The shadow has been met.
The child has been heard.
The story has been reclaimed.
The light has returned.

And now a new chapter begins —
written by a whole soul,
with a steady heart,
standing in fullness,
and walking forward unafraid.

THE
SHADOW &
LIGHT TOOLS

Part One: Illumination – The Shadow Mirror

If You're Struggling

A note for anyone who feels slow, stuck, or unsure

Shadow healing can stir deep layers of feeling, memory, and instinct.
Some days you may feel clear and strong.
Other days, nothing moves — or emotions rise and fall like waves.

If you're struggling, please hold these truths close:

Healing is not linear

Progress doesn't follow a straight path.
It loops, spirals, pauses, and unfolds in layers.

Sometimes growth looks like:

- clarity
- release
- breakthroughs

And sometimes it looks like:

- silence
- rest
- emotional fog
- distraction

- difficulty accessing your memories
- numbness

All of these are normal.

Your body opens only at the pace it feels safe.

Plateaus are wisdom, not failure

When things feel "stuck," it's often because your nervous system is integrating.

Just like a bone that begins to mend,
there is a stillness phase where the body reorganizes itself quietly.

Plateaus mean:

- your system is adjusting
- your identity is reshaping
- your inner child is deciding it can trust you

Nothing is wrong.

Tears are release, not regression

Tears, shakiness, or emotion surfacing do not mean you're "back there."

They are signs that:

- tension is loosening
- unspoken truth is being acknowledged
- the body is letting go

Many people cry not from pain,
but from relief.

If memories come slowly, that's protection

When the body doesn't reveal details immediately,
it's because it is prioritizing stability.

Your nervous system is deciding what you are ready for.
It will not show more than you can hold.

Trust its intelligence.

Feeling tired is normal

Shadow work can bring fatigue because:

- emotional tension is unwinding
- the nervous system softens
- your body is integrating new beliefs

Rest is part of the healing cycle.

Sleep, quiet, and stillness are medicine.

You are not meant to do this perfectly

There is no required level of emotion, memory, or
breakthrough.

Healing does not measure worth.

Just showing up to witness yourself
is already a transformation.

When nothing is moving... something still is

Even when you feel "blocked,"
shadow work can be reorganizing the deep structure of your
inner world.

Sometimes the biggest shifts happen silently —
noticeable only weeks or months later.

Be gentle with the timing.

Your nervous system is leading the way

Your body is not fighting you.
It is protecting you.

It slows down when:

- emotions are too large
- inner safety feels uncertain
- integration is incomplete
- the inner child needs reassurance

This is intelligence, not resistance.

The parts of you that once survived
are still guarding you —
and your compassion teaches them how to stand down.

If you feel heavy or tender

Place a hand on your heart and quietly say:

"I'm here.
I'm safe.
I don't need to rush."

Your body will hear you.

Healing is not measured by speed

It is measured by:

- self-understanding
- emotional spaciousness
- softness toward the past
- inner safety
- freedom to be who you are
- calm in the body

These are subtle… but they are everything.

Even small shifts — like breathing deeper, speaking more honestly, or noticing a trigger without collapsing — are monumental.

Please remember this most of all

If you are struggling,
you are in the part of healing that matters most:

the part where you stay with yourself
even when it is hard.

You did not abandon the child you once were.
You are learning to hold them.

That alone rewrites the story.

You are not behind.
You are not failing.
You are not "stuck."

You are becoming. Slowly. Wisely. Beautifully.
At a pace that protects you.

If You Need Support: A Note About Professional Guidance

Shadow work is powerful, sacred, and deeply human.
And while much of this journey can be walked with self-reflection, journaling, and energy practices, there are times when the inner world asks for companionship, support, and a trained witness.

There is no weakness in needing help.
In fact, reaching out is often the most courageous part of healing.

When Professional Support Can Help

Consider speaking with a counselor, therapist, trauma-informed practitioner, or specialist if you notice any of the following while doing this work:

• intense emotional activation that feels bigger than what you can hold alone
• memories emerging with confusion, panic, or overwhelming physical responses
• dissociation, numbness, or shut-down
• old coping mechanisms becoming strong again
• feelings of isolation, hopelessness, or fear

These experiences don't mean you're failing.
They're signals that your nervous system is asking for more safety, structure, and support than the page alone can provide.

Your Story Deserves to Be Witnessed With Care

Some shadows began in silence.

You don't need to heal them in silence.

A trained professional can help you:

• process memories without retraumatization
• identify emotional patterns with clarity
• gently challenge self-blame or confusion
• build grounding skills
• hold space for grief, truth, or unanswered questions

Healing is easier when someone knowledgeable and compassionate is beside you.

Energy Work & Psychology Can Work Together

Shadow work through Reiki, meditation, journaling, and somatic practices can be profoundly transformative — but it does not replace mental health care.

Both can work beautifully together.

Think of it like this:

- Counseling helps you understand the story and its effects.
- Energy work helps the nervous system release the emotional imprint of that story.

Together, they support the mind, the body, and the spirit in becoming whole.

If You Are Unsure

If a part of you wonders, *"Should I get help?"*
that is already a sign to at least explore the idea.

Many people seek support not because they are broken, but because they are wise enough to know they deserve to heal safely.

A Final Reassurance

Seeking professional help is not a sign that your shadow is "too much."

It means your healing matters.

It means your pain is worthy of tenderness.

It means your inner child deserves guidance that honors their story.

Whether you walk this path alone or accompanied, this truth remains:

You are already doing something brave.
You are turning toward yourself instead of away.

If at any moment these pages become too heavy, too confusing, or too painful — pause, breathe, and reach for support.

There is strength in that choice.
And there is light in every step you take.

Which Archetype Lives In You?

A reflection guide for recognizing your shadow pattern with compassion.

Throughout this book, we explored four foundational shadow archetypes that commonly emerge from childhood experiences:

1. The Silent Child
2. The Watcher
3. The Protector
4. The Disappearing Self

Many people see themselves in one more than the others — but it is just as common to see pieces of all four.

This appendix is designed to help you identify your dominant pattern, not as a label, but as a mirror.

The goal is not diagnosis.
It is recognition — so that you can meet yourself with clarity, tenderness, and truth.

HOW TO USE THIS

1. **Notice, don't judge.**
   These archetypes are reflections, not verdicts.
2. **Be curious.**
   Ask yourself:

- *Which pattern appears most often in me?*
- *When does it activate?*
- *What does it protect?*

3. **Separate identity from strategy.**
   The archetype is not *who* you are —
   it is how you learned to stay safe.
4. **Recognize the gift beneath the wound.**
   Every archetype carries extraordinary strengths once
   freed from fear.
5. **Return to compassion.**
   Shadow healing begins when you see yourself with
   tenderness.

THE HEART OF THIS GUIDE

If you recognize yourself in any of these archetypes —
it means you survived something that required instinct, wisdom,
sensitivity, and emotional intelligence far beyond your years.

The shadow you formed is not weakness.

It is proof of how brilliantly you adapted.

And the moment you begin meeting these parts of yourself with
compassion…

your shadow stops feeling like a burden
and starts becoming your medicine.

THE SILENT CHILD

"I learned that quietness kept the peace."

You may resonate with this archetype if, as a child or adult, you
notice patterns like:

- hesitating to speak up
- feeling safer when blending in
- keeping opinions to yourself

- minimizing your emotional needs
- staying quiet during conflict
- avoiding attention
- being called "good" or "easy" as a child

Core wound:
Speaking once felt risky.

Core gift:
When healed, your voice becomes powerful because you speak from depth, truth, and insight.

THE WATCHER

"I learned to see everything, so nothing could surprise me."

You may align with this archetype if you:

- sense emotional shifts before others notice
- read body language, tone, and energy instinctively
- scan the room or atmosphere for safety
- anticipate reactions
- rarely take words at face value
- feel uneasy in unpredictable environments

Core wound:
Safety once depended on vigilance.

Core gift:
Your intuition is sharp, accurate, and spiritually attuned — an extraordinary tool once released from fear.

THE PROTECTOR

"I learned to take care of others, even when no one took care of me."

Signs you may carry this archetype:

- emotional caretaking feels automatic
- you try to soothe, fix, counsel, or mediate
- you feel responsible for others' feelings
- you apologize often
- you feel guilty when you cannot help
- you step into leadership roles quietly

Core wound:
You believed peace depended on you.

Core gift:
You become a natural healer, guide, and wise emotional leader when boundaries return.

THE DISAPPEARING SELF

"I learned to stay small so I could stay safe."

You may see yourself in this archetype if:

- you comfort yourself by withdrawing
- independence feels safer than needing others
- you tend to minimize your desires
- you feel invisible or overlooked
- attention makes you uneasy
- emotional overwhelm makes you retreat inward

Core wound:
Visibility once felt threatening.

Core gift:

Your depth, imagination, empathy, and emotional wisdom run profoundly deep — and become luminous when allowed expression.

IF YOU SEE MORE THAN ONE

That is normal — even expected.

Many people developed multiple archetypes at different stages of childhood, depending on:

- who was in the room,
- the emotional climate,
- the relationships involved,
- and the instincts that arose moment to moment.

This guide is not meant to confine you.

It is meant to help you understand your survival patterns with compassion.

Because the child who learned to speak softly, watch closely, protect others, or disappear…

was doing their absolute best with what they had.

Mapping Your Archetype Across Life

Where does your shadow pattern appear today?

This page helps the reader recognize how their childhood survival strategy shows up in modern life.

It is not meant to judge or label.
It is simply a mirror.

THE PURPOSE OF THIS MAP

It is not meant to reveal weakness.

It is meant to show how brilliantly the inner child survived —
and how those strategies now reveal your intuitive gifts.

Silence becomes discernment.
Awareness becomes intuition.
Caretaking becomes leadership.
Disappearing becomes inner depth.

Every archetype carries both wound and wisdom.

And when recognized,
they become sacred tools
instead of unconscious patterns.

Place marks, words, or sentences under any area that applies.

RELATIONSHIPS

In relationships, do I tend to:

- shrink or silence myself (Disappearing Self / Silent Child)
- sense emotional changes quickly and react inwardly (Watcher)
- soothe, fix, or carry the emotional labor (Protector)

Prompts:

- When conflict arises, what is my first response?
- Do I share my needs openly?
- Do I seek peace even at the expense of my truth?

PARENTING

With children, do I:

- watch intensely to keep them safe (Watcher)
- over-function emotionally (Protector)
- minimize my needs or voice to keep calm in the home (Disappearing Self / Silent Child)

Prompts:

- Do I avoid conflict or discomfort?
- Do I carry guilt when I can't meet every need?
- Do I sense their emotions before they speak?

WORK & CAREER

At work, do I:

- stay quiet even when I have valuable ideas (Silent Child)
- observe environments deeply and pick up interpersonal dynamics (Watcher)
- take on tasks or emotional weight that isn't mine (Protector)
- avoid attention or visibility (Disappearing Self)

Prompts:

- Do I step back even when I'm qualified?
- Do I take care of others more than myself?
- Do I feel uneasy being seen or recognized?

FRIENDSHIPS

With friends, do I:

- listen more than I speak
- support others but rarely share my own struggles
- sense when someone is hurting even without words
- disappear when I feel emotionally overwhelmed
- keep peace rather than express discomfort

Prompts:

- Who do I feel safest being emotionally open with?
- Where do I still hold back?

SPIRITUALITY

In spiritual spaces, do I:

- carry intuitive sensing I rarely speak about
- observe humanity with depth and empathy
- feel like an emotional guide or silent healer
- retreat inward to find meaning
- feel called to serve or protect others

Prompts:

- When does intuition speak loudest?
- What spiritual gifts developed because of childhood shadow patterns?
- How does healing my shadow change my relationship with the Divine?

The Freezing Responses Wheel

Understanding Your Nervous System's Wisdom

When a child feels unsafe — emotionally, physically, or energetically — the nervous system instinctively creates strategies to survive.

These survival responses are not "overreactions," flaws, or personality defects.
They are *automatic, physiological safety codes* developed in the body long before conscious thought existed.

In shadow healing work, recognizing these patterns brings compassion, clarity, and release.

The four primary responses are:

- Fight
- Flight
- Freeze
- Fawn

Every child uses at least one of them — often more than one — depending on the environment.

And each response naturally shapes the shadow archetypes discussed in this book.

The Four Responses & Their Archetype Mirrors

1. Freeze → The Disappearing Self

Primary instinct:
"Become small. Stay still. Don't be noticed."

Freeze is the body's deep instinct to shut down emotional expression and physical presence when the threat feels too big or unpredictable.

Common signs:

- emotional numbness
- blanking out
- shutting down during conflict
- holding still, inwardly collapsing
- going "invisible"

Shadow Archetype Connection:

- *The Disappearing Self*

Children in freeze learn:

- disappear to survive
- do not take up space
- become silent in the moment of danger

This response later shows up as self-minimizing, avoidance, hiding opinions, or retreating inward.

2. Fawn → The Protector

Primary instinct:
"Keep them calm. Take care of them. Make yourself useful."

Fawning is not weakness.
It is the nervous system's attempt to soothe the threat by becoming emotionally accommodating or helpful.

Signs:

- caretaking others
- reading moods to keep peace
- fixing emotional tension
- apologizing quickly
- taking responsibility that isn't yours

Shadow Archetype Connection:

- *The Protector*

Children who fawn become emotional mediators.
They learn that compassion and caretaking soften danger — and bring a sense of control.

The gift beneath the wound:
These children grow into natural healers, leaders, and empaths once they learn boundaries.

3. Flight → The Watcher

Primary instinct:
"Detach, step back, stay alert, observe everything."

Flight isn't always physical.
It often shows up as emotional distance, hypervigilance, or scanning the environment for changes.

Signs:

- sensing danger first
- mentally checking out
- emotionally leaving the situation
- always watching, anticipating
- reading subtle shifts in tone, energy, or posture

Shadow Archetype Connection:

- *The Watcher*

Children in flight become internal observers.
They learn safety comes from awareness, prediction, and distance.

Their gift becomes extraordinary intuition and perception — once it's not powered by fear.

4. Fight → The Silent Child (Collapsed Expression)

Primary instinct:
"Do nothing that escalates danger. Still yourself. Keep the peace."

Many assume "fight" means anger or aggression.
In childhood, fight can also collapse inward — where the instinct isn't to lash out, but to suppress expression to prevent conflict.

Signs:

- silencing feelings
- swallowing truths
- self-censoring
- holding emotional tension inside
- staying neutral to avoid conflict

Shadow Archetype Connection:

- *The Silent Child*

Instead of outward fight, the child fights internally — suppressing their voice as a way to prevent escalation.

The gift:
When healed, the Silent Child becomes an honest, powerful communicator whose words carry depth, empathy, and truth.

Why This Wheel Matters

Seeing childhood coping patterns through the lens of nervous system survival changes everything.

Instead of:

- "I'm broken."
- "Why am I like this?"
- "I should be stronger."

It becomes:

- "My body protected me."
- "My instincts were intelligent."
- "I adapted exactly as I needed to."

This is the doorway to compassion.

You Were Never Weak

Freeze, Flight, Fawn, Fight —
these responses were not flaws.

They were:

- brilliance
- instinct
- emotional intelligence
- safety mechanisms
- survival strategies

And the shadow archetypes that grew from them were not "damage."
They were genius adaptations in a small, vulnerable body that needed protection.

Now as an adult, you get to reshape them consciously:

- Freeze can become presence.
- Fawn can become empathy with boundaries.
- Flight becomes intuition rather than hypervigilance.
- Fight becomes calm truth and secure communication.

Your shadow patterns existed because something in you wanted to live.

The nervous system chose the path that kept you safe long enough to reach this moment — reading these words, breathing steadily, reclaiming yourself.

That is not brokenness.
That is triumph.

Reflection Prompts

Use these to explore your patterns gently:

1. Which response do I recognize most often?

---

2. When did I first learn it?

---

3. What was I trying to prevent, avoid, or protect?

---

4. How did this response keep me safe as a child?

_____

5. How can this same instinct become a strength as an adult?

_____

_____

A Final Reminder

You are not the child who froze.
Or watched.
Or carried others.
Or went silent.

You are the adult who survived.

Your shadow responses were wisdom written into your body for protection,
and now you are learning how to reclaim their power without living in their fear.

That is healing.

Where My Voice Froze

A Reflection for Returning to Your Truth

Many shadow patterns begin in the moment a child realizes that speaking their truth, asking for help, or expressing a feeling might lead to conflict, rejection, danger, or shame.

The voice doesn't disappear overnight —
it slowly freezes.

First as caution.
Then as instinct.
Eventually as identity.

This exercise helps you recognize where that moment began, so that you can help your voice thaw — gently, at its own pace.

There is no need for full clarity or memory.
Even a feeling, a tone, or a single moment is enough.

You are not reliving the past —
you are reclaiming the right to speak.

Before You Begin

Take a slow breath.

Place one hand on your heart or throat.

Tell the child within you:
"You are safe to remember only what feels light."

Nothing here needs precision.
Shadows are emotional landscapes, not court records.

What matters is the *felt sense* of when silence became safety.

Guiding Prompts

You may write in full sentences, single words, or fragments of memory.

1. What is the earliest moment I remember feeling unsafe to speak?
(Was it a tone? A look? A reaction? A rule?)

_____

_____

2. Was there someone whose anger, silence, unpredictability, or sadness made me feel like speaking might hurt me?
Who was I afraid to upset?

_____

_____

3. What topics or emotions felt "dangerous" to bring up?

_____

_____

4. Did I ever swallow my truth to protect someone else?
(Parent, sibling, authority figure, younger child?)

_____

_____

5. When did I first learn that silence brought peace, safety, or acceptance?

_____

_____

6. Did I ever feel invisible because speaking felt unsafe?

_____

_____

7. If my voice made someone uncomfortable, how did they react?

_____

_____

_____

Gentle Awareness Questions

These are not for blame — only clarity.

⬦ Who did I most need to feel safe with?

_____

⬦ Whose comfort did I protect with my silence?

_____

◇ What did silence prevent?
(shame, punishment, conflict, anger, withdrawal, punishment, chaos?)

_____

◇ What was I trying to keep intact?

_____

_____

Reframing the Freeze

Finish this sentence slowly, compassionately:

"My silence wasn't weakness — it was _____."
(Home. Shield. Protection. Instinct. Intelligence.)

_____

Then complete this one:

"Today, I am learning that my voice is _____."
(Allowed. Safe. Worthy. Strong. Sacred.)

_____

_____

For the Heart

Your voice froze for a reason.

Not because you were timid, flawed, or passive.

It froze because:

- your nervous system was brilliant
- your intuition was accurate
- and your heart was trying to keep you alive in its own way

Silence, for the child you once were, was wisdom.

Now, for the adult reading these words, voice can become power.

You do not need to shout.
You do not need to prove.
You do not need to battle.

You only need to breathe truth back to the place that once held fear.

Even a whisper is healing.
Even a single honest sentence can thaw decades of quiet.

Your voice never left you.
It simply waited for safety.

And every word you speak now —
to yourself, to your memories, to your healing —
is a return to wholeness.

The Shadow Origin Map

Tracing where your patterns began — and why they made sense at the time.

Every shadow trait once served a purpose.

It kept you safe, connected, unseen, unnoticed, compliant, invisible, helpful, quiet, scanning, or alert — because at some point, those patterns were the safest way to exist.

This page helps you explore how your environment shaped the version of you that learned to protect itself.

Move slowly.
Answer only what feels safe.
You are not looking for blame — only understanding.

These questions are doorways.
They reconnect you to truth with tenderness.

1. ATMOSPHERE OF THE HOME

What did the emotional climate feel like when you were young?

Check any words that resonate, or write your own:

- tense
- quiet
- unpredictable
- controlled
- chaotic
- heavy
- sad
- secretive

- sharp or explosive
- withdrawn
- emotionally absent
- affectionate
- calm
- warm
- confusing
- mixed signals

Describe it in your own words:

_____

_____

_____

The atmosphere of the home is often the first sculptor of the shadow.

2. THE EMOTIONAL RULES

Every family has spoken and unspoken emotional "rules."

These shape how a child learns to express, shrink, protect, or become silent.

Reflect gently:

- What emotions were safe to express?
- Which emotions were forbidden or punished?
- What behaviors were expected from you?

Examples to guide you:

- "Don't cry."
- "Don't be loud."
- "Don't upset anyone."
- "Smile and keep peace."
- "Don't speak against adults."
- "Pretend everything is normal."
- "Don't talk about the truth."

List any emotional rules you absorbed:

_____

_____

_____

These rules often become survival strategies that follow us into adulthood.

3. WHO HELD POWER?

Children instinctively learn who is safe, unpredictable, sensitive, neglectful, volatile, or emotionally fragile.

Reflect gently:

- Who controlled the atmosphere?
- Who did you feel you needed to tiptoe around?
- Who did you feel responsible for soothing?

This isn't about blame —
it's about recognizing where your survival instincts were formed.

_____

_____

_____

When a child identifies power dynamics, they shape their personality around them.

4. WHAT EMOTIONS WERE "ALLOWED"?

Some children were allowed to feel freely.
Others learned to suppress everything.

Complete these prompts:

- It felt safe to show:
  _____
- It felt dangerous to show:
  _____
- When I expressed emotion, the response usually was:
  _____

This is where many shadow patterns begin.

5. WHAT BEHAVIORS FELT SAFER?

Shadow traits usually reflect the behaviors that reduced risk.

Which survival pattern protected you?

(check any that apply)

- staying quiet
- being overly helpful
- reading others constantly

- shrinking into the background
- perfectionism
- emotional numbness
- avoiding attention
- always being "good"
- caretaking the adults
- hiding feelings
- anticipating danger
- people-pleasing
- walking on eggshells

Shadow patterns didn't appear randomly.
They were intelligent, instinctive responses to emotional reality.

Write any that come to mind:

_____

6. WHERE DID YOU HIDE PARTS OF YOURSELF?

Children will bury:

- anger
- sadness
- joy
- curiosity
- voice
- needs
- dreams
- vulnerability

if they believe those parts threaten their safety.

Ask yourself gently:

- What parts of me did I learn to hide?
- Which sides of me felt unwelcome?

- Where did my spirit go when it didn't feel safe?

_____

_____

_____

Those hidden parts are often the wisest, most sensitive, most spiritual pieces of the self.

They did not die.
They went quiet until it was safe to return.

WHY THIS MAP MATTERS

When you understand the landscape that shaped your shadow...

- shame dissolves,
- clarity rises,
- compassion replaces self-judgment.

You stop asking "What's wrong with me?"
and begin asking:

"What happened to me that made this pattern necessary?"

Shadow traits become evidence of survival, not flaws.

They reveal:

- who you were protecting,
- what you were defending,
- and how much wisdom lived inside you even as a child.

This map is not meant to reopen pain —
it is meant to validate the brilliance of your adaptations.

You survived by instinct.
You shaped yourself around what was real at the time.

And now, with understanding and safety,
those patterns can soften.

Because your body knows
danger is no longer here.

And the light inside you
is ready to return.

Emotional Rules of the Home

The Invisible Codes That Shaped Your Shadow

Every childhood environment carries emotional rules.
Some are spoken directly.
Most are silently absorbed.

They form through tone, body language, reactions, expectations, and atmosphere.
And even if no one said them aloud, the child learns them as survival laws.

This page is a space to recognize those unwritten codes — not to blame, but to understand.

Because shadow traits always make sense when seen in the context that shaped them.

How to Use This Page

1. Sit quietly and breathe slowly.
2. Let memories surface without force.
3. Write down the emotional "rules" that seemed to govern your home.
4. Include both spoken and unspoken rules.
5. Be honest and gentle — you are remembering, not reliving.

There are no right answers.
Only your truth.

Examples of Emotional Rules

These are patterns commonly found in homes that create shadow traits:

Rules about Emotions

- "Do not upset anyone."
- "Stay quiet during conflict."
- "Don't cry."
- "Pretend everything is normal."
- "Never talk about what happens here."
- "Good children are silent children."

Rules about Safety

- "Do not wake them."
- "Stay out of the way."
- "Watch carefully for mood changes."
- "Know when to disappear."

Rules about Responsibility

- "Keep the peace."
- "Make sure others are okay."
- "Your job is to be 'good.'"
- "Avoid being a problem."

Rules about Truth

- "What you feel might not be real."
- "Your perception is incorrect."
- "Don't question adults."
- "Your instincts are overreactions."

Rules about Identity

- "Do not take up space."
- "Blend in."
- "Be strong. Do not need help."
- "Stay small to stay safe."

These internal laws rarely vanished in adulthood — they simply went underground and began shaping relationships, decisions, and self-worth.

That's why naming them brings power back to your hands.

Your Emotional Codes

Use this space to write what you learned silently:

In my home, it felt like the rules were:

_____

_____

_____

_____

_____

_____

_____

_____

Reflective Prompts

1. Which of these rules still influence me today?
(For example, silence in conflict, caretaking, shrinking, perfectionism)

_____

2. Where did I see these rules most?
(At the dinner table? When someone was angry? During uncertainty?)

_____

3. Did any rule feel protective at the time? If so, how?

_____

4. What do I know now — as an adult — that the child could not have known then?

_____

_____

A Gentle Truth

Children do not create emotional rules by mistake.

They create them with brilliant precision.

Because the child understands:

- which actions bring calm
- which tone means danger
- which silence keeps peace
- which shrinking prevents hurt

Those rules were survival intelligence.

And now, as adults, they can be seen clearly — not as identities but as strategies that were once necessary.

Once named, they no longer need to control.

You can take what protected you
and reshape it into wisdom.

You are no longer living inside those rules.
You are the one who writes new ones.

Journaling Prompts for Shadow Integration

Gentle questions to help you uncover patterns, stories, and strengths.

Write slowly.
Answer honestly.
Allow memories to surface at their own pace.

These prompts are meant to bring clarity — not pain.

Use them as doorways, not excavations.

1. Safety & Expression

- When I was a child, what moments made me go silent?
- What kinds of emotions did I feel unsafe expressing?
- Who did I believe it was safest to be around?
- When did I first learn that speaking might bring consequences?

2. Awareness & Intuition

- What were the earliest signs that I could sense emotional shifts?
- Did I learn to read facial expressions, tone, or subtle body language?
- What did I notice about others that no one talked about out loud?

3. Responsibility

- Did I ever feel responsible for other people's happiness?

- In what ways did I try to "fix" or soothe others?
- Did I feel older than my age, emotionally?

4. Visibility

- When did I feel safest being quiet, small, or unseen?
- What did I fear might happen if I took up space?
- Have I ever minimized myself to avoid conflict or attention?

5. Patterns in Adulthood

- How do I react today when someone is upset or angry?
- When do I stay quiet even though I want to speak?
- What situations trigger my instinct to disappear, fix, or observe?

6. Compassion

- If I met my younger self today, what would I tell them?
- What do I understand now that I didn't understand then?
- What strengths did that child carry that I still have?

Childhood Story Recall Page

For those ready to safely remember and witness their story.

This page offers a structured way to hold early memories with tenderness.

You are not required to remember everything.
You are simply invited to listen to the echoes.

Recall only what feels safe.
Stop anytime your body becomes tense or overwhelmed.

Part I — Early Atmosphere

- What did my childhood home feel like emotionally?
- Was it silent? Chaotic? Gentle? Tense?
- How did people communicate? Through words, tone, silence, energy?

Part II — First Memories of Instinct

- What is the earliest moment where I remember:
    o freezing,
    o watching,
    o hiding,
    o caretaking,
    o or shrinking?
- What did I fear would happen if I didn't respond that way?

Part III — Confusion & Beliefs

- As a child, what beliefs did I take on about myself?
    o Was it "I must not cause trouble"?

- o "I need to make everyone comfortable"?
- o "I don't matter"?
- o "Speaking makes things worse"?

Part IV — The Body's Memory

- Does my body recall anything my mind does not?
- Do certain places, sounds, tones, expressions, or smells trigger emotions?
- Where does tension sit in my body when I think of childhood?

Part V — The Meaning I Hold Today

- Looking back with adult wisdom:
  - o What do I know now about those moments?
  - o What was the child in me trying to protect?
  - o What strength was developing in the shadows?

Leave space for pauses.
For tears.
For blank pages.
For silence.

Sometimes remembering is not about clarity —
but compassion.

What My Body Learned

How the Nervous System Carries the Shadow

Long before a child understands danger,
their body does.

When emotions felt unpredictable, unspoken, or overwhelming,
the nervous system adapted by storing patterns in posture,
breath, muscle tone, and vigilance.

These patterns often remain into adulthood — not because the
past is still alive, but because the body was never told it could
stop protecting you.

This page invites you to listen respectfully to your body's
wisdom — not as evidence of trauma, but as proof of how hard
it worked to keep you safe.

The body remembers what the child could not say.

Where the Shadow Lives in the Body

Shadow responses show up in subtle ways:

Posture

- rounded shoulders
- head lowered
- chest drawn inward
- attempt to make oneself smaller

Breath

- shallow inhalation

- holding breath unconsciously
- upper chest breathing instead of full belly expansion

Muscle Tension

- jaw locking
- stomach tightness
- throat constriction
- rigid shoulders
- fists, arms, or legs tightening

Hyper-Awareness

- scanning rooms
- reading tone, energy, or facial expressions instantly
- bracing before anything actually happens

Emotional Tone Sensitivity

- detecting conflict before words are spoken
- shrinking in response to subtle shifts in mood
- feeling danger in silence, not sound

These are not "problems."
They are embodied intelligence.

They once protected you.

And now they can guide you toward healing.

Gentle Body Awareness Prompts

Use these questions without urgency.
Even vague sensations count.

1. Where in my body do I feel tension when I think of childhood?
(Stomach? Chest? Throat? Jaw? Legs? Shoulders?)

---

2. Do I notice any physical patterns when I feel emotionally unsafe?
(shrinking, crossing arms, holding breath, freezing stillness)

---

3. When I think of being small, what sensations arise?
(warmth? tightness? numbness? tremor? pressure?)

---

4. Do I feel my emotions more in the chest, stomach, throat, or somewhere else?

---

5. Did I hold my breath as a child?
If so, do I still do it now without noticing?

---

6. Do I brace my body before conflict, discomfort, or uncertainty?

_____

7. What posture did I adopt to stay safe in childhood?
(invisible, quiet, folded inward, always alert, sitting near doors, watching adults)

_____

_____

Energy Medicine Insight

In shadow healing, the body tells the story through:

- aura pressure
- chakra contraction
- breath blocks
- muscular locking
- emotional numbness
- freeze response

For many survivors of instability, intuition sharpened because the body became an antenna — sensing danger faster than the mind.

This is why much of the "shadow energy" is found in:

- the solar plexus (identity, shame, responsibility)
- the heart chakra (emotional closure)
- the throat chakra (muted expression)
- the root chakra (safety)

You already teach that energy moves through breath, presence, intention, and frequency.

Here, you're showing the reader that their body learned to hold energy in specific ways because it was trying to protect them.

There is no flaw in that.

Only deep wisdom.

Integration Prompts

◊ What is my body still trying to protect me from?

◊ What does my body believe silence or tension prevents?

◊ What part of me still thinks safety means being small, still, quiet, or watchful?

◊ If I could tell my body one truth it never heard as a child, what would it be?

A Truth to Hold Close

Your body is not your enemy.
It is your oldest protector.

Tense muscles once meant safety.
Shallow breath once meant control.
Stillness once meant invisibility.
Scanning once meant survival.

We do not shame the body for learning these things.

We thank it.

And then, through reiki, grounding, breath, and compassionate awareness, we teach it something new:

"I am safe now."
"You can rest."
"We don't need to shrink to survive."

Because healing doesn't erase the past —
it changes the body's relationship to it.

Your body deserves the same peace your soul has been seeking.

My First Sacred Gift

Recognizing the Light That Was Born in the Shadow

Shadow work is not only about uncovering pain.
It is about discovering the brilliance that grew beneath it.

Every child who learned to survive also learned something
extraordinary —
a gift that emerged from instinct, sensitivity, and emotional
intelligence.

This page helps you identify the first sacred gift that was
forming in you long before you understood its purpose.

Your gift was not taught.
It awakened.

It came from necessity.
And now it is part of your spiritual power.

Shadow as Seed — Light as Growth

Many gifts begin inside shadow patterns:

- silence becomes depth
- vigilance becomes intuition
- caretaking becomes compassion
- disappearing becomes reflection
- fear-awareness becomes discernment
- emotional sensitivity becomes healing wisdom
- hyper-observation becomes spiritual insight

What once protected you
is now the very source of your inner medicine.

You did not just survive.
You grew.

You became someone with perception, empathy, strength, and emotional clarity well beyond your years.

That was your first sacred gift.

Common Gifts Born from the Shadow

You may recognize one or more of these in yourself:

- Empathy — sensing emotional reality beyond words
- Intuition — feeling truth before it is spoken
- Discernment — reading intentions, energy, and environment
- Insight — seeing dynamics others overlook
- Awareness — understanding tone, silence, and atmosphere
- Creativity — inner worlds as a refuge and source of meaning
- Self-Preservation — instincts that kept you safe
- Emotional Intelligence — knowing what others feel without being told
- Compassion — attunement born from sensitivity
- Leadership — mediating, calming, or guiding others
- Resilience — the capacity to endure and evolve
- Spiritual Sensitivity — sensing deeper truths beneath reality

Every one of these traits is a form of brilliance forged in shadow.

They are the light that grew without permission, instruction, or praise.

They grew because your soul is stronger than anything that ever tried to silence it.

Reflection Prompts

Answer gently and honestly — fragments and feelings are enough.

1. What survival instinct became one of my strongest gifts as an adult?
(Sharp intuition? Pattern reading? Emotional attunement?)

_____

_____

2. What qualities did I develop because I had to stay aware, quiet, or perceptive as a child?

_____

_____

3. Which shadow trait evolved into spiritual intelligence?
(Watching became discerning. Silence became wisdom. Stillness became presence. Sensitivity became empathy.)

_____

_____

4. What skill or awareness do I have today that most people do not?

_____

_____

5. If my inner child could see who they became, what gift would they be proud of?

_____

_____

_____

Completing the Circle

Finish these softly — the words matter less than the intention.

"The shadow taught me to _____."
(see deeply, feel truth, protect others, listen with my whole body…)

_____

"And today that gift helps me _____."
(guide, heal, create, lead, nurture, intuit…)

_____

_____

A Final Truth

Your sacred gift did not come from the wound —
it came from the intelligence that formed inside it.

The shadow was only the soil.

The gift was the seed.

And you carried that seed forward
into adulthood, spirituality, purpose, and calling.

You did not just survive your childhood —
you transformed it.

Your light was already forming
in the moments you stayed quiet, watched closely, sensed
deeply, or protected others.

You were becoming
before you even knew it.

Whatever gift formed there, nurture it now.
It has been with you since the beginning.

How to Know When to Pause

A Safety Guide for Shadow Healing

Shadow work can be deeply clarifying —
but it can also stir old nervous-system memories.

Healing is not meant to feel like emotional flooding or collapse.
It should be steady, compassionate, and paced by your safety.

This page helps you recognize when to pause, rest, and ground
so the work remains gentle and supportive.

There is no prize for pushing through discomfort.
Your body sets the pace — and that pace is sacred.

WHEN TO PAUSE YOUR PRACTICE

If any of the states below arise,
it is time to stop, breathe, and return another day.

1. Dissociation

• feeling far away from your body
• drifting, foggy thinking
• blurry senses
• observing rather than feeling present

This means your nervous system is protecting you by
disconnecting.
Pause immediately.

2. Overwhelm

• emotions feel too big
• mental chatter speeds up
• inability to focus
• a sense of "too much at once"

Overwhelm is the body asking for smaller steps.

3. Emotional Numbness

• total lack of feeling
• emotional flatness
• no connection to memories or words

Numbness is not failure —
it is the freeze response.
It signals that you need grounding before continuing.

4. Panic or Terror Sensations

• racing heart
• chest tightness
• trembling
• sense of danger
• rapid breath

Panic is a sign that the shadow is being approached too quickly.
Your body needs time and stabilization.

5. Spiraling or Collapsing Thoughts

• catastrophic beliefs
• self-blame
• confusion
• mental loops

This is the mind trying to "solve" emotional content.
Pause and return to presence.

6. Emotional Collapse

• sudden exhaustion
• crying without relief
• feeling powerless
• shutting down

Collapse is the body saying "I need rest, not more process."

Pausing Is Not Regression

It is maturity.

It means you are listening to your nervous system
instead of forcing your inner work.

Shadow healing should feel like:

- guided curiosity,
- careful witnessing,
- gentle release
  —not emotional overwhelm.

Your system is learning safety.
Safety requires pacing.

WHAT TO DO WHEN YOU NEED TO PAUSE

1. Stop the practice immediately

Close the journal, rest your hands from Reiki, end visualization, stop breathwork.

Give your body stillness.

2. Ground

Choose one of the following:

- feet flat on the floor
- touch something solid (table, chair, ground)
- hold a soft object
- feel your breath in your belly

Say quietly:

"I am here.
I am safe.
This moment is mine."

3. Orient to the present

Look around the room slowly.

Notice:

- colors
- objects
- light
- textures

This tells the brain:
"The past is not happening now."

4. Breathe

Long exhales regulate the nervous system faster than anything else.

Even four slow breaths are enough.

5. Hydrate

Sip water to reconnect with physical reality.

6. Return Later

Not tomorrow if that feels too soon.
Not next month if you're not ready.

Healing waits for you.
It never expires.

Important Reminder

You never need to push through pain here.

Shadow work touches delicate inner landscapes.

Pausing is profound self-care —
the same care the child within you always needed.

A Checklist for Safety

Before continuing any practice, ask:

* Do I feel steady in my body?
* Is my breath slow and low?
* Can I stay present without bracing?
* Do I feel a sense of inner safety?

If the answer is "no" to any of these,
wait.

Your healing is not strengthened by force —
only by compassion.

When Professional Support May Help

If pauses become frequent
or inner work consistently brings panic, numbness, or collapse,
it may mean the body needs a guide beside you —
not because you are weak,
but because your story deserves tenderness and skill.

A trauma-informed counselor, therapist, or energy healer
can help hold the edges safely.

You do not need to walk into the shadow alone.

A Truth to Keep Close

Healing is not a straight line.
It is a tide.

Sometimes the body opens.
Sometimes it closes.

Both are wisdom.

When you pause, you honor:

- the child who endured,
- the nervous system that survived,
- and the adult who now chooses safety over urgency.

The shadow does not need force to release.
It needs presence, breath, and time.

And stopping is often the moment when true healing begins.

Part Two: Transformation – The Light Tools

Grounding Rituals for After Shadow Release

How to Return to the Body With Safety and Presence

Shadow work softens emotional defenses, loosens tension, and allows long-held energy to rise to the surface.

This is healing —
but the body needs grounding afterward.

Not because anything is "wrong,"
but because the nervous system has just done something profound:

It allowed truth to move.

Grounding tells the body:

- the moment is complete,
- safety is still present,
- and everything can settle.

These rituals help you integrate the experience gently, close energetic portals, and return fully to the present.

Use them anytime you finish journaling, breathwork, Reiki, or any emotional processing.

Let them be slow, simple, nurturing.

1. Feet on the Floor

Sit with both feet flat — barefoot if possible.

Feel weight.

Notice:

- soles against the ground
- gravity
- temperature
- texture

Breathe into the belly.

Silently repeat:

"I am here.
I am safe.
I am present in my body."

This is one of the fastest ways to stabilize the nervous system after emotional work.

2. Salt Bath or Salt Shower

Salt has been used in spiritual traditions for centuries to cleanse emotional residue and reset energetic fields.

Add sea salt, Epsom salt, or Himalayan salt to a bath.

If you prefer a shower, sprinkle salt in your hands and let water wash it away.

Set a soft intention:

"What no longer belongs to me is released."

Let warmth, salt, and water become the closure of the session.

3. Hold Something Soft

Shadow work often activates the need for comfort — especially for the inner child.

Hold:

- a pillow
- a blanket
- a stuffed animal
- a soft scarf

Notice the weight and texture.

It signals to the body:
"Tenderness is safe now."

4. Warm Herbal Tea

Choose calming herbs:

- chamomile
- lavender
- lemon balm
- holy basil
- peppermint

Warmth moves energy downward, calms the vagus nerve, and helps the emotional body settle.

Sip slowly.

Let the warmth drop from the chest to the belly.

5. Sit Under a Tree

Nature reorganizes the nervous system instinctively.

Trees especially are grounding:

- roots
- stillness
- silence
- presence

Lean your back against the trunk if possible.

Visualize your energy moving downward into the earth.

Let the body feel held.

6. Earthing

Walk barefoot on:

- grass
- soil
- sand

Place hands on natural surfaces:

- stone
- wood

- river rock

Earthing discharges excess energy and recalibrates the body's electrical field.

Even 3 minutes can be enough.

7. Singing Bowl at the Root Tone

A low, steady frequency near the root chakra range (110–150 Hz range) helps stabilize the base of the spine and the nervous system.

Let the sound vibrate through your bones.

Imagine it anchoring you to the earth.

8. Weighted Blanket or Gentle Pressure

A small weight over:

- chest
- stomach
- hips

can calm emotional activation.

Pressure signals to the brain:
"You are contained.
You are safe.
You are here."

9. Place a Hand on the Root or Heart

If emotions still swirl, place one hand over the root (base of spine) or heart.

Breathe slowly.

Invite grounding:
"I return to myself.
I am steady."

10. Eat Something Nourishing

Food — especially grounding foods — brings you back into the physical body.

Examples:

- potatoes
- warm soup
- oats
- rice
- root vegetables

Chew slowly.

Let nourishment replace tension.

Integration Prompts

If you feel called, journal one or two of the following:

⋄ How do I feel physically right now?

⋄ What emotion softened or shifted?

⬧ Did I notice any warmth, pressure, or release in my body?

⬧ What do I need in this moment to feel safe and complete?

A Final Note

There is no "emotional vulnerability" here —
only openness.

Your body has just done something remarkable:

- it softened
- it remembered
- it released
- it trusted

Grounding rituals complete that cycle.

They tell the nervous system:
"Nothing is unfinished.
I am safe now.
I am fully here."

Let these practices be your closing doorway
after every moment of shadow work.

Because healing isn't only about releasing the past —
it is also about rooting into the present.

Shadow Release Breathwork

Teaching the Body That It Is Safe to Let Go

When the body has lived in fear, silence, or vigilance, one of the hardest things to learn is that safety is now present.

Shadow release isn't only emotional or energetic —
it is physiological.

Because the nervous system decides whether:

- memories surface,
- emotions soften,
- tension unwinds,
- and energy unhooks from the past.

Breath is the most direct way to communicate safety to the body.

Not by forcing calm,
but by sending a biological message:
"You can soften. I am safe."

This method is designed specifically for shadow work —
to prepare the body, soothe the nervous system, and allow release with peace rather than pressure.

WHY BREATH MATTERS IN SHADOW HEALING

Many people don't realize that childhood coping patterns are stored in breath:

- shallow inhalation
- held breath

- tight ribs
- tense diaphragm
- throat constriction

These are survival imprints.

Shadow breathwork gently unravels these signals and replaces them with new ones:

- grounded presence
- internal safety
- emotional permission
- nervous system rest

Breath tells the body what the mind cannot.

CORE PRINCIPLES OF THE SHADOW RELEASE BREATH

1. Low Belly Activation
    Safety is signaled when breath drops lower into the abdomen and pelvis.
    Shallow chest breathing mimics danger.
2. Elongated Exhale
    A longer exhale activates the parasympathetic nervous system —
    the physiological gateway to softness and release.
3. Gentle Holding Points
    Pausing briefly at the heart or root gives the body a felt experience of grounding and presence.
4. No Forcing
    This breath is slow, natural, and subtle.
    Tension means pause, not push.
5. Integration, Not Catharsis
    The goal is not emotional flooding.
    It is somatic permission.

Shadow Release Breath Sequence

You may read through once, then repeat slowly with your eyes closed.

Step 1: Connect to the Low Belly
Place one hand on your lower abdomen, the other over your heart.
Breathe in slowly through the nose, guiding breath down to the belly.

Let it expand gently — even if it's only a little.

Inhale silently:
"I am safe in my body."

Step 2: The Heart Pause
At the top of the inhale, pause for 1–2 seconds.
Soften the chest.
Let the heart expand.

This pause teaches the body:
"I can hold emotion without bracing."

Step 3: Long Exhale Through the Mouth
Exhale twice as slowly as the inhale.
Let the body release weight and tension with the breath.

Whisper or think:
"I let go of what I no longer need."

Step 4: Root Connection
On the next breath, imagine the inhale traveling down the spine.
As you exhale, gently contract the pelvic floor — as though grounding the breath downward into the earth.

This brings safety awareness into the root chakra and nervous system.

Step 5: Repeat 5–8 Breath Cycles
Slow.
Gentle.
Never rushed.

Feel:

- weight dropping,
- shoulders loosening,
- belly expanding,
- breath deepening.

Even a few slow breaths can melt decades of vigilance.

Optional Add-On for Emotional Release

If emotions begin to surface gently — pressure in the chest, tightness in the throat, warmth in the solar plexus — place one hand on the area.

Breathe into it with kindness, not urgency.

Say inwardly:

*"Thank you for protecting me.
You may rest now."*

This teaches the body that release is safe.

Not dramatic.
Not demanded.
Just allowed.

IF YOU FEEL RESISTANCE

Resistance is not failure.
It is proof that your body took its role very seriously.

If the breath stays shallow, or tension tightens:

- slow down
- shorten the breath
- return to the root

Tell your body the truth it waited decades to hear:

"I am here with you.
You do not need to guard me anymore."

WHEN TO USE SHADOW RELEASE BREATHWORK

It is an ideal companion to:

- inner child journaling
- archetype recognition
- Reiki sessions
- cord dissolution work
- emotional retrieval practices

Use it:

- before processing memories
- after release rituals
- before sleep
- during activation
- anytime you feel contraction

It is the bridge between "remembering" and "healing."

WHAT THE BREATH TEACHES THE SHADOW

Slow, grounded breath tells the nervous system:

- I belong here.
- I can feel without danger.
- I can remember without collapsing.
- I can open without harm.

It replaces survival coding with presence.

Breath is the language of the body.
Safety is the message.
Release is the outcome.

A SOFT CLOSING THOUGHT

The child you once were learned to guard the breath —
to shrink it, hide it, hold it, tighten it.

The adult you are now can teach it to open again.

Feel the belly expand.
Feel the heart soften.
Feel the root settle.
Feel yourself return.

Shadow healing is not forcing light in.
It is breathing space into the places that feared it.

One inhale at a time.
One exhale at a time.

That is how the shadow learns to rest.

The Shadow & Light Reiki Sequence

A guided energetic process for releasing emotional imprints, restoring coherence, and reuniting the inner child with the adult self.

The Shadow & Light Reiki Sequence is a focused energetic ritual designed specifically for shadow healing.

Instead of treating the body symptom-by-symptom, it works through the emotional layers stored in the:

- aura
- chakras
- nervous system
- subconscious memory
- inner child

This sequence is gentle, never forced, and deeply intuitive. It supports the energetic release of past pain while helping the body feel safe enough to integrate the light of truth.

It can be performed on yourself or offered to clients — but always slowly, compassionately, and at the body's pace.

SAFETY FIRST

Before beginning, understand this:

Shadow release is not extraction.
It is permission.

We are not removing anything "bad."
We are acknowledging what once protected us,
and inviting it to relax.

If emotional intensity rises during any step:

- pause,
- breathe,
- ground,
- or return to the root chakra.

Healing is not a race.

The body decides the pace.

HAND PLACEMENTS FOR EMOTIONAL RELEASE

*Starting at the head and moving downward, we guide light
through the shadow's most common holding centers.*

Each position is held for 2–5 minutes
(or longer if intuition calls for it).

Placement 1: Third Eye — Releasing Over-Watching
Place both hands gently across the forehead.

Purpose:

- soften hypervigilance
- calm over-awareness
- dissolve frozen scanning patterns
- release "anticipating danger" programs

Invite:
"I see the world clearly now.
I no longer need to watch for what once frightened me."

Placement 2: Temples — Unwinding Stored Confusion
Hands cup both temples.

Purpose:

- ease emotional memory circuits
- calm looping thoughts from the past
- release childhood "interpretation errors"

Invite:
"I understand now what I could not understand then."

Placement 3: Back of Head — Releasing Freeze Imprints
Hands cradle the base of the skull.

Purpose:

- dissolve immobilization responses
- unfreeze emotional paralysis
- restore presence to the body

Invite:
"It is safe for me to be present in my own life."

Placement 4: Throat — Returning Expression
Hands over the throat.

Purpose:

- release swallowed words
- heal silence patterns
- reawaken safe communication

Invite:
"My voice is safe.
My truth is safe.
I am safe being heard."

Placement 5: Heart — Inner Child Reconnection
Hands directly over the chest.

Purpose:

- soften emotional numbness
- heal disconnect from self
- restore the ability to feel

Invite:
"I am worthy of love, compassion, connection, and tenderness."

Placement 6: Solar Plexus — Reclaiming Self
Hands over the diaphragm.

Purpose:

- release self-blame
- dissolve generational shame
- restore personal power
- heal identity distortions

Invite:
"I am not the cause of what once hurt me.
I am the result of what I survived."

Placement 7: Sacral — Emotional Memory Clearing
One hand over the lower abdomen, the other over the pelvis.

Purpose:

- release emotional residue from childhood
- heal vulnerability barriers
- dissolve imprints around innocence or safety

Invite:
"My emotions belong to me.
My inner child is safe in this body."

Placement 8: Root — Grounding, Safety & Connection
Hands at the tailbone/sits bones
(lying down is easiest).

Purpose:

- release survival fear
- reestablish embodied safety
- calm nervous system
- stabilize presence

Invite:
"I am safe now.
I belong in this world.
The ground holds me."

THIRD EYE & HEART INTEGRATION

To harmonize intuition and emotional truth, place one hand on the forehead and one on the heart at the same time.

This creates a bridge between:

- perception and compassion
- memory and truth
- intuition and feeling

It allows the body to reinterpret past events without emotional panic.

The nervous system learns:
"I can see clearly *and* feel safely."

This pairing is one of the most healing positions in shadow Reiki work.

It softens old beliefs like:

- "My feelings weren't valid."
- "I misunderstood everything."
- "I cannot trust myself."

And replaces them with:

- self-trust,
- emotional wisdom,
- and intuitive confidence.

ROOT CHAKRA GROUNDING

Every shadow sequence must end at the root.

Without grounding, emotional release can feel destabilizing.

At the root, visualize:

- weight
- warmth
- gravity
- earth
- anchoring
- breath settling low in the body

Allow the energy to descend downwards rather than swirl upward.

Shadow healing is about stability, not catharsis.

The root anchors that truth.

Invitations for grounding:

- "I am in my body."
- "I am safe in the present moment."
- "I do not need to disappear to be safe."
- "I stand on solid ground."

SOLAR PLEXUS RECLAIMING

The solar plexus is where the most common shadow distortions live:

- self-doubt
- self-blame
- hyper-responsibility
- guilt
- identity confusion
- internalized shame

Energy work here helps the inner child surrender beliefs such as:

- "It was my fault."
- "I wasn't enough."
- "I should have been different."
- "I caused their pain."
- "I should have stopped it."

Reclaiming the solar plexus restores:

- identity
- worth
- autonomy
- core confidence
- emotional sovereignty

Most people feel a noticeable shift after this placement —
as though the center of gravity returns to the body.

HOW TO SELF-HEAL SAFELY

This sequence is gentle, but shadow energy can be tender.

Simple precautions ensure healing stays peaceful:

1. Go slowly

Spend more time on the areas that feel tense, numb, emotional, or heavy.

2. Stop if you feel overwhelmed

Tears are normal — panic is not.

If the body goes into fight-flight:

- pause
- breathe
- return to the root

3. Finish the full sequence

Especially end with grounding.

Shadow release without grounding can feel emotionally open or unsteady.

4. Hydrate

Water helps clear energetic residue and restore coherence.

5. Journal

Write down whatever surfaced:

- sensations
- memories
- phrases
- emotions
- beliefs

Even if it doesn't make sense.

Especially if it doesn't make sense.

The shadow often speaks in symbols before clarity forms.

WHEN TO REPEAT

You can do this sequence:

- monthly
- during emotionally triggering periods
- after breakthroughs
- before major changes
- as inner-child work
- as gentle maintenance

Healing is not repetition of pain.
It is repetition of presence.

THE HEART OF THIS SEQUENCE

Shadow healing is not about "removing darkness."

It is about witnessing what the child once carried alone…

and saying:

"You are safe now.
You are seen.
You are understood.
You are allowed to be whole."

Reiki brings frequency
to the places that froze.

Warmth
to the places that went numb.

Truth
to the places that held confusion.

Light
to the places that feared it.

And through that union of shadow and light,
the aura reorganizes itself into coherence.

The child inside you and the adult you have become
finally stand together in the same moment.

Seen.
Safe.
Whole.

Aura Cleansing & Protection Practices

Integration, Sovereignty & Energetic Reorganization

After shadow work, the aura becomes more open, receptive, and permeable.
This is not fragility — it is the energetic equivalent of softened armor.

When the nervous system relaxes,
when emotional imprints loosen,
when truth rises into consciousness...

the field shifts.

These practices help the aura stabilize, reorganize, and strengthen so you leave every session whole, clear, and centered.

Protection here is not about fear, defence, or threat.
It is about sovereignty —
the gentle declaration:

"My energy is mine, and it is safe within me."

WHY AURA INTEGRATION MATTERS AFTER SHADOW WORK

Shadow healing:

- releases stored emotion
- dissolves identity distortions
- softens freeze responses
- opens the heart field
- shifts internal frequency

This can make the aura feel:

- thinner
- more spacious
- more sensitive
- more permeable

Integration practices help the aura re-form around the true self, not the shadow self.

They also support the chakras as they recalibrate from survival mode into presence.

SIMPLE & GENTLE PRACTICES

(No force. No fear. Just reorientation.)

1. Aura Sweeping

Run your hands slowly around your body, 3–6 inches away from the skin.

Move from head → down to feet.

Imagine brushing away:

- tension
- residue
- emotional static

End with flicking motions away from the body.

This isn't "removing darkness."
It's clearing old impressions that no longer belong.

2. Golden Edge Visualization

Close your eyes and imagine a soft gold light forming at the outer edge of your aura.

Not a shield.
A boundary of truth.

Warm, gentle, permeable to love —
but naturally closed to anything that does not align with clarity, peace, or safety.

Whisper inwardly:

"My field is whole.
My energy is my own."

3. Reiki through the Aura

Hover your palms around the body — especially:

- belly
- heart
- throat
- back of the head
- root

Allow Reiki to run through the auric layers rather than directly on the skin.

Feel:

- warmth
- tingling
- subtle flow

Imagine the aura smoothing, brightening, and reorganizing itself as the nervous system settles.

4. The Hand Sweep at the Heart

Place your palm flat at the center of your chest.

Sweep outward slowly while exhaling.

Let the body release any emotional pressure or leftover heaviness that rose during the work.

Repeat 3–5 times.

This helps close the session emotionally and energetically.

5. Breath Sealing

Inhale through the nose into the belly.
Exhale through the mouth while gently visualizing the aura contracting back to its comfortable size.

When shadow work is active, the aura often expands.

This breath seals the field, not with walls, but with coherence.

At the end, say:

"I return fully to myself."

6. Grounded Hand Positions

Two placements that restore energetic clarity:

Heart + Root
One hand at the chest, one over the lower belly or base of spine.

This harmonizes emotional truth and safety.

Third Eye + Solar Plexus

One hand on the forehead, the other on the diaphragm.

This integrates perception with identity — powerful after shadow insights.

Allow energy to run gently for 1–3 minutes.

7. Simple Sovereignty Affirmations

Speak or think one of the following:

"My aura is whole and clear."
"My energy belongs only to me."
"I am present, grounded, and safe."
"I release what is not mine with compassion."

These are not defenses —
they are declarations of identity.

No force.
Just truth.

Energetic Insights for the Reader

After shadow release, many people feel:

- lighter
- softer
- more emotionally exposed
- more intuitive
- more attuned

This is normal.

It means the aura is reorganizing itself around your healed identity rather than your survival identity.

Cleansing practices help the field recalibrate and return to a coherent, grounded state.

INTEGRATION PROMPTS

Write what comes without judgment:

1. How does my aura feel after doing shadow work?
(larger, softer, warmer, quieter, open?)

_____

2. What parts of my field feel sensitive or tender?

_____

3. Which practice above brings the most peace to my body?

_____

4. What affirmation resonates most today?

_____

_____

A CLOSING THOUGHT

Aura cleansing after shadow work is not a barricade —
it is a blessing.

It says to the child within:
"You are safe now.
Your energy is your own."

It says to the adult:
"You can carry your light without shrinking."

And it teaches the field:
to reorganize around peace,
clarity,
identity,
and sovereignty.

Your aura is not fragile —
it is radiant.

These practices help it remember.

How To Perform Cord Dissolution

(Step-by-Step)

A simple, grounded structure that anyone can use.

1. Identify the root imprint

Ask gently:

- What belief formed around this memory?
- What did the child decide about themselves?
- What fear settled into the body?

Examples:

- "I am unsafe."
- "I must stay small."
- "If I speak, I'll be hurt."
- "It was my fault."
- "I am responsible for others."

This belief *is the cord.*

2. Place one hand on the solar plexus

This is where identity, self-definition, and internalized blame sit.

Breathe deeply.

Say quietly:
"I know why you believed this."

This validates the intelligence of the child —
and removes shame from the imprint.

3. Ask the body if the belief is still necessary

Not mentally — but intuitively.

Does the nervous system still respond with:

- tension?
- fear?
- contraction?
- shrinking?

Honesty matters more than logic.

Even a false belief can feel true if the body still remembers it.

4. Send Reiki to the belief itself

Rather than trying to erase it, offer warmth, safety, and
frequency.

Shadow dissolves through gentleness — not force.

Imagine the belief softening inside the solar plexus:

- untangling
- loosening
- melting
- unhooking

Because beliefs dissolve when the body recognizes they are no
longer required for survival.

5. Speak the Release Truth

This is the energetic cord's undoing.

Examples:

"I release the belief that I was responsible for what happened."
"I let go of the need to stay small to stay safe."
"I no longer carry guilt that was never mine."
"I return this fear to its origin with compassion."

You are not cutting the cord.
You are dissolving it by replacing the old story with truth.

6. Invite the inner child out of the contract

Say inwardly (or aloud):

"You do not need to hold this anymore.
I am safe now.
I can protect us.
You are free."

This step is essential.

The belief did not form in the adult mind —
it formed in the child.

Only the child's energy can release it.

7. Finish at the Root Chakra

Place both hands over the base of the spine.

Imagine warmth and grounding running downward into the earth.

Because when the root feels safe, the past loosens immediately.

The root chakra tells the nervous system:
"There is no threat here.
We are home now."

And the cord dissolves.

Emotional Deprogramming Pages

Anchoring Truth After the Shadow Releases

When a belief formed in childhood dissolves, it leaves space.
Space that once held fear, shame, confusion, or false identity.

That space must be filled on purpose.

Because if we do not consciously anchor a new belief,
the nervous system often reaches back for the familiar —
even if the familiar was painful.

This section helps you rewrite the internal laws that shaped you,
gently replacing survival programs with truths that support:

- safety
- worth
- presence
- self-love
- personal identity

It is not about erasing the past —
but about choosing what defines you now.

WHY EMOTIONAL DEPROGRAMMING MATTERS

Shadow beliefs were created to keep you safe.
They were based on the information a child could understand.

Examples:

- "If I stay quiet, no one gets hurt."
- "I'm responsible for their feelings."
- "I must stay small to survive."

- "My needs don't matter."
- "I am the cause of the pain around me."

These beliefs dissolve when shadow healing takes place.
But the nervous system needs to learn something new:

"I am safe now.
I am worthy now.
I am allowed to exist fully now."

Emotional deprogramming transforms the inner child's worldview
into the truth the adult now lives.

HOW TO USE THESE PAGES

1. Identify the belief that once protected you.
2. Honor the intelligence behind it.
3. Replace it with a truth that reflects your healed identity.
4. Repeat that truth until the body recognizes it as safe.

Let the shift be slow and compassionate.

This is not forcing a new mindset.
It is teaching the body a new emotional language.

PART ONE: NAMING THE OLD BELIEF

Begin by writing the belief that developed in childhood —
the one that shaped your shadow pattern.

Examples:

- "I shouldn't speak."
- "I must make everyone comfortable."
- "I'm safest when unseen."

- "Conflict means danger."
- "Other people's feelings are my responsibility."

What belief did the child in me adopt?

_____

_____

_____

PART TWO: HONORING ITS PURPOSE

Every belief exists for a reason.

How did this belief protect me as a child?
(What outcome did it prevent? What peace did it preserve?)

_____

_____

What danger did this belief help me navigate?

_____

_____

When you see the wisdom in the belief,
the nervous system relaxes
instead of resisting the shift.

_____

PART THREE: CHOOSING THE NEW TRUTH

Write a belief that reflects who you are now, as an adult with agency, boundaries, and self-awareness.

Examples:

- "My voice is safe."
- "I am not responsible for others' emotions."
- "It is safe to take up space."
- "I choose visibility without fear."
- "My needs matter and deserve to be spoken."
- "I can stand in conflict without losing myself."

What truth replaces the old belief?

_____

_____

Make sure it feels grounded —
not forced affirmation,
but emotional reality.

_____

PART FOUR: TEACHING THE BODY

The body must feel the new truth to accept it.

Place a hand on the solar plexus or heart
and imagine the belief sinking into the nervous system with breath.

Complete these sentences to let it anchor:

"My new truth feels safe because..."

_____

_____

"My body can trust this now because..."

_____

_____

PART FIVE: REMEMBERING WHO I AM BECOMING

Shadow healing is not only about release.
It is transformation.

Finish with these reflections:

"The old belief protected me when I was small.
The new belief supports me as I grow because..."

_____

_____

"I am becoming someone who..."

_____

_____

SAMPLE REFRAMES

To show the reader what this process looks like:

Old Belief:
"If I stay quiet, everything stays calm."
New Truth:
"I can speak truth gently and still be safe."

Old Belief:
"I must carry everyone's emotions."
New Truth:
"I am responsible only for my energy."

Old Belief:
"I'm safer when unseen."
New Truth:
"My presence is allowed, welcomed, and worthy."

Old Belief:
"Conflict means danger."
New Truth:
"I can remain grounded and present in uncomfortable moments."

These truths do not erase history —
they liberate the identity shaped by it.

A FINAL NOTE FOR THE HEART

When you rewrite emotional belief,
you are not dishonoring the child you once were.

You are completing their work.

They built the survival program.
You are writing the freedom code.

This is how shadow turns to light:
not through denial,
but through evolution.

Say gently to the inner child:

"You kept me alive.
Now I will teach us how to live."

Chakra-by-Chakra Shadow Release Guide

A Map of Where the Shadow Lives in the Energy Body

Shadow imprints do not live only in memory or emotion — they organize themselves through the energetic system.

Each chakra holds fragments of:

- beliefs,
- unspoken truths,
- emotional echoes,
- survival patterns,
- nervous system reactions,
- and childhood interpretations.

This guide helps you recognize where those patterns may be stored, and how to gently dissolve them through awareness, breath, intention, and Reiki.

Use this as a quick reference during healing, reflection, or integration.

HOW TO USE THIS GUIDE

1. **Scan inwardly during shadow work.**
   Notice which chakra tightens, contracts, or feels heavy.
2. **Place the hand gently over that center.**
   Reiki, warmth, and presence help the imprint loosen.
3. **Breathe into the space.**
   Long exhales let stored fear unwind.
4. **Speak the new truth aloud.**
   Identity replaces survival.

5. Ground at the root before closing.
   Always return to the body.

Root Chakra

Shadow Themes:

- fear
- survival mode
- instability
- danger memory
- shrinking
- hyper-arousal at sudden sounds
- difficulty trusting safety

Why These Imprints Form:
When childhood never felt deeply secure, the nervous system wired safety into stillness, vigilance, or withdrawal.
The root remembers these cues long after the danger is gone.

Gentle Clearing Suggestions:

- grounding breath into the pelvis
- walking barefoot on earth
- hand at the tailbone while repeating
  "I am safe in the present."
- slow Reiki flow at the base of the spine

Sacral Chakra

Shadow Themes:

- shame
- distrust in worthiness
- innocence wounds

- confusion around body safety
- difficulty receiving affection
- emotional withdrawal

Why These Imprints Form:

When vulnerability felt risky, the sacral closed as a form of protection.
It often holds the emotional imprint of not feeling fully safe to be soft, expressive, or childlike.

Gentle Clearing Suggestions:

- hand over lower abdomen with slow exhale
- soft hip movements (circular or rocking)
- warm baths for emotional permission
- affirmation:
  "My emotions belong to me, and they are safe."

Solar Plexus

Shadow Themes:

- identity distortion
- self-blame
- internalized guilt
- responsibility for others' feelings
- "it was my fault" programming
- loss of self-trust

Why These Imprints Form:

Children often fill in missing information with self-blame.
When adults lacked emotional regulation, the child absorbed the responsibility.

Gentle Clearing Suggestions:

- place hands over diaphragm
- dissolve false beliefs through breath
- Reiki flow here first during cord dissolution
- mantra:
  "I was never the cause.
  I am worthy as I am."

Heart Chakra

Shadow Themes:

- emotional numbness
- distrust of closeness
- fear of vulnerability
- believing love is conditional
- self-protection through detachment

Why These Imprints Form:
When emotional safety was uncertain, the heart learned to close
— not as rejection, but preservation.

Gentle Clearing Suggestions:

- hands over the heart until warmth rises
- slow inhale directly into chest space
- gratitude for the inner child's wisdom
- affirmation:
  "I am worthy of tenderness, connection, and love."

Throat Chakra

Shadow Themes:

- silence
- swallowed truth
- self-erasure
- avoiding conflict
- minimizing needs
- cautious speech

Why These Imprints Form:
The throat remembers every moment where silence felt safer than truth.
Shadow here forms when speaking once felt dangerous, unwelcome, or disruptive.

Gentle Clearing Suggestions:

- palm at the throat while breathing slowly
- humming or toning softly
- whispering truths aloud
- mantra:
  "My voice is allowed.
  My truth is safe now."

Third Eye Chakra

Shadow Themes:

- hypervigilance
- scanning environments
- predicting danger
- misinterpreting neutrality as threat
- difficulty trusting intuition

Why These Imprints Form:

When peace was unpredictable, perception became the child's safety tool.
The third eye became a constant observer, reading what others missed.

Gentle Clearing Suggestions:

- hand across the brow
- Reiki to soften vigilance
- low-belly breathing to anchor awareness
- affirmation:
  "I see clearly now.
  I no longer need to watch for danger."

Crown Chakra

Shadow Themes:

- spiritual doubt
- disconnection
- feeling unsupported by life
- questioning self-worth in the universe
- feeling "unprotected"

Why These Imprints Form:

If caretakers were emotionally inconsistent, the crown mirrors that uncertainty — translating human instability into spiritual mistrust.

Gentle Clearing Suggestions:

- hand at the crown or hovering above head
- visualizing light descending
- gratitude statements
- prayer, meditation, or stillness

- affirmation:
  "I am connected to something greater than my past."

A CLOSING INSIGHT

Shadow imprints are not signs of damage —
they are energetic memories of instinct.

Each chakra tells a story:

- where you protected yourself,
- where you shrank,
- where you held emotion,
- and where wisdom quietly formed.

The moment you approach these places with light, softness, and
Reiki —
they begin to reorganize.

You do not force open what once closed.

You breathe into it.
You listen to it.
You honor it.
And it melts.

This is how chakra work becomes shadow work:
not through awakening what is broken —
but through returning love to what once feared it.

Post-Shadow Emotional Care

How to Support Yourself After Deep Inner Work

After shadow release, the emotional body and nervous system often continue reorganizing long after the session ends.

This is not regression —
it is integration.

When the body finally feels safe enough to soften, the layers that once held fear, silence, or tension may unwind for hours, days, or weeks in subtle ways.

This page helps you understand and support your internal landscape as it recalibrates.

You are not "falling apart."
You are coming back together.

COMMON EXPERIENCES AFTER SHADOW WORK

These responses are normal, healthy, and often signs that integration is happening.

1. Emotional Tenderness

You may feel softer, more vulnerable, more sensitive, or more spacious inside.

This is the nervous system moving from defense into openness.

It is safe to feel tender.

Let the body rest in it rather than closing again.

2. Dreams Resurfacing

Shadow work dissolves suppression.
Some dreams may replay events, symbols, emotions, or
metaphors connected to your story.

Dreams are how the subconscious:

- reorders memory
- reinterprets history
- releases stored energy
- makes meaning

They are not warnings.
They are integration.

3. Memories Appearing Slowly

Fragments may show up:

- in images,
- in feelings,
- as passing thoughts,
- or vague emotional impressions.

This does not mean something "new" happened to you —
it means your body trusts you enough to let the past be
witnessed with clarity.

Let memories be symbolic rather than literal if that feels safer.
Your healing is not dependent on precision.

4. Deep Fatigue

Energetic release and emotional softening can feel like a long
exhale after years of bracing.

Fatigue is often the body saying:
"I can finally rest."

Sleep longer.
Move slower.
Drink more water.

Your system is transitioning out of survival mode.

5. Somatic Release

Shadow work can loosen what once stayed locked.

You may notice:

- heat
- trembling
- belly tightness
- pressure in the chest
- throat constriction
- tingling
- waves of sadness or relief

These are nervous system decompressions —
stored emotion exiting through the body.

Breathe gently and stay present.
Nothing is wrong.

HELPFUL WAYS TO SUPPORT YOURSELF

1. Lower the Stimulation

Give your senses softness:

- dim lights
- quiet spaces
- gentle sounds
- looser clothing

Intense emotional processing needs stillness to settle.

2. Move Slowly

Integration is not done through action.
It is done through presence.

Short walks, stretching, or warm baths help the body reorganize energy without overwhelming it.

3. Hydrate and Nourish

Emotional release affects breath, muscles, and the nervous system.
Hydration and warm, grounding foods help re-stabilize the body.

4. Journal Briefly

Even one sentence can anchor clarity.

Questions to explore:

- What softened?
- What surfaced?

- What truth am I sitting with now?

You do not have to explain — just witness.

5. Rest During Waves

If emotions rise, allow them.

Shadow healing does not require revisiting pain —
only acknowledging whatever needs a moment to move
through.

If tears come, let them.

If stillness calls, honor it.

6. Small Comfort Rituals

Wrap yourself in a blanket
Drink warm tea
Sit in sun or near a window
Hold something soft

These actions speak directly to the body:
"You are safe."

WHEN TENDERNESS FEELS NEW OR STRANGE

If being open feels unfamiliar,
remind yourself:

"This is what healing feels like."

The body may be cautious at first —
it spent years in vigilance or contraction.

Softness needs practice.

IF MEMORIES SURFACE LATER

Some shadow fragments rise only when the body is rested, supported, and unguarded.

This does not mean you missed something.

It means you are ready now in a way you were not before.

Always meet memories with:

- breath
- grounding
- compassion
- and the understanding that they are echoes, not threats.

INTEGRATION REMINDER

Shadow work is not meant to leave you "open" indefinitely.

Your body naturally re-forms energetic coherence and emotional grounding when you:

- breathe deeply
- connect to the root
- rest
- hydrate
- do something nurturing
- place a hand on your heart

Your system returns to balance because safety is no longer conditional.

A FINAL TRUTH FOR PEACE

Shadow work is not a destabilizing force.

It is the body finally telling the truth —
slowly, gently, with wisdom.

Emotional tenderness is softness replacing armor.
Dreams are the mind returning clarity to old stories.
Fatigue is proof that protection can rest.
Somatic release is stored past unhooking from the present.

You are not unraveling.

You are integrating.

Your system is remembering itself without fear.

Let it be slow.
Let it be tender.
Let it be sacred.

And always return to this reality:

The past is not here.
You are safe in your life now.
Your body is learning that with you.

Signs of Integration

How to Know When Healing Is Taking Root

Shadow work can feel tender, emotional, and unfamiliar.
And many people wonder quietly:

"Am I actually healing...
or just stirring things up?"

Integration rarely looks dramatic.
It usually shows itself in small shifts —
changes of breath, emotional distance, inner calm, softness.

This page helps you notice those quiet markers.

You're not meant to chase transformation —
only to recognize it when it arrives.

1. Emotional Distance From Painful Memories

You may still remember what happened,
but emotional charge lessens.

The body stays soft.
Your breath stays open.
Your heart remains accessible.

The memory becomes information — not tension.

This is healing.

2. Remembering Without Contraction

When you think of childhood or past experiences,
your body stays present:

- shoulders loosen
- chest stays open
- stomach doesn't tighten
- throat doesn't close

You witness rather than relive.

That's integration.

3. Triggers Feel Lighter

Situations that once activated vigilance, guilt, or fear now cause
only mild discomfort — or none at all.

Maybe you pause, breathe, notice the old impulse…

…but you choose a different response.

That moment of choice is progress.

4. Breath Stays Low in the Body

After working through the shadow, breath begins to drop
naturally into the belly and ribs.

Chest breathing and held breath become less automatic.

The nervous system is learning:
"I don't need to brace anymore."

5. The Voice Feels More Free

You speak more honestly,
even gently.

You name boundaries,
needs,
truths.

Not dramatically —
just with calmness and certainty.

The throat chakra is releasing its old instinct of silence.

6. Reflexive Guilt Softens

When someone is upset,
you no longer assume:

- "It's my fault."
- "I caused this."
- "It's my job to fix it."

You breathe.
Observe.
Stay grounded.

Responsibility returns to its rightful home.

That is integration.

7. Boundaries Feel Calm & Natural

You say:

- "No"
- "Not right now"
- "That doesn't feel aligned"

without panic,
and without needing to defend or explain.

Truth becomes a neutral statement rather than a threat.

8. Compassion Toward Yourself Appears Spontaneously

Moments that would once trigger shame, self-judgment, or harsh inner criticism are now met with softness:

- "Of course that hurt."
- "I understand why I reacted that way."
- "I was doing my best."

Self-kindness arrives without effort.

9. Curiosity Replaces Fear

You begin asking:

- "What did this moment awaken?"
- "What belief is speaking here?"
  instead of:
- "What's wrong with me?"
- "Why can't I handle this?"

Curiosity is peace taking shape.

10. Your Nervous System Recovers Faster

Even if you feel triggered,
you return to presence more quickly:

- breath slows
- the body relaxes
- thoughts clear

Emotion rises,
but does not hijack.

Your system knows the way home.

11. You Feel Yourself Growing Bigger Inside

Not louder.
Not hardened.

Simply more spacious,
more grounded,
more like the person you were meant to become.

The shadow stopped defining you.
It began educating you.

12. You Sense a Quiet Reclaiming

Integration often sounds like:

- "I'm allowed to be here."
- "I don't need to disappear."
- "I'm not responsible for everything."
- "I trust myself now."

Identity is returning to its true form.

13. You Feel Safe Being Present in Your Own Body

This may be the most powerful sign of all.

You no longer float,
brace,
scan,
or shrink.

You exist.

Fully.

Here.

What Integration Is Not

It is not:

- perfection
- never being triggered
- remembering every detail
- eliminating emotion

Integration means:
"The past no longer owns my nervous system."

Healing doesn't erase what happened.
It transforms your relationship with it.

REFLECTION PROMPTS

Notice the subtle shifts:

Which signs above do I recognize in myself?

Where do I feel more space, peace, or softness than before?

What small moments proved I've changed?

Where do I still feel tender, and can I honor that gently?

A Quiet Celebration

Integration is rarely loud.

It feels like:

- breathing more deeply
- speaking a truth without shaking
- feeling warmth in your chest
- remembering something painful without collapsing
- showing compassion to your younger self

These are not small things.

They are milestones.

And they are proof that shadow work is not breaking you open
—
it is putting you back together.

One breath, one insight, one softened moment at a time.

You do not have to rush.

Healing is already happening.

Example Shadow Healing Session Layout

A gentle step-by-step flow for emotional release, energetic unwinding, and inner-child integration

This layout is not a rule.
It is simply a supportive rhythm — one that honors the natural intelligence of the body and nervous system.

Move slowly.
Stop anytime you feel overwhelmed.
Repeat steps when needed.
Let intuition lead.

1. Grounding Breath

Begin by signaling safety to the body.

Suggested options:

- slow belly breathing
- elongated exhales
- inhale through the nose, exhale through the mouth
- one hand on the heart, one on the root

Purpose:

- settle the nervous system
- soften vigilance
- remind the body that the present moment is safe

Stay here until breath feels slow, steady, and anchored.

2. Gentle Observation of Emotion or Memory

Once settled, allow whatever is present to arise:

- a feeling
- a sensation
- a memory
- a belief
- an image
- or simply a heaviness in the body

You do **not** need full clarity.
Shadow work often begins as a whisper, not a headline.

Ask quietly:

- "What is this feeling protecting?"
- "Where do I feel this in my body?"
- "What belief is attached to this memory?"

No searching.
No forcing.
Only witnessing.

3. Shadow Release Hand Placements

Move through the placements slowly and intuitively:

1. **Third Eye** — softening over-watching
2. **Temples** — unwinding confusion
3. **Back of Head** — melting freeze responses
4. **Throat** — returning voice
5. **Heart** — reconnecting to the inner child
6. **Solar Plexus** — releasing self-blame and distortion
7. **Sacral** — clearing emotional residue

8. Root — restoring safety

Hold each position 2–5 minutes, longer if needed.
Whisper healing truths as you go.

4. Cord Dissolution on the Belief

When a belief becomes clear — even partially — it is ready to soften.

Steps:

1. place one hand at the solar plexus
2. identify the belief (e.g., "I had to stay small")
3. validate its origin ("I know why you believed this")
4. offer Reiki to the belief itself
5. speak the Release Truth
6. invite the inner child out of the contract

Remember:
You are not *cutting* the cord.
You are dissolving it with compassion and truth.

The body releases what it decides is no longer required for survival.

5. Integration Statement

Anchor the new truth with intention.

Examples:

- "I am safe now."
- "My voice matters."
- "I am not responsible for what wounded me."
- "I choose truth over fear."

- "I keep the wisdom, not the wound."
- "I belong to myself."

Say it slowly.
Repeat it until your body softens.
This step rewires identity.

6. Root Chakra Grounding

Always finish here.

Hands at the base of the spine.
Warm breath down into the belly and hips.

Visualize:

- weight
- earth
- gravity
- steady presence

Invite:

- "I am here."
- "I am safe."
- "I live in the present."
- "My body is my home."

When the root is grounded,
the inner child relaxes,
and integration settles peacefully.

7. Journaling Reflection

End with gentle written reflection:

Suggested prompts:

- What surfaced?
- What softened?
- Where did emotion shift?
- Did any beliefs reveal themselves?
- How does my body feel now?
- What compassion do I have for my younger self?
- What truth do I want to carry forward?

The purpose is not analysis.
It is witnessing.

Writing makes healing *conscious*.
It helps the new identity take root.

Session Notes

- You may move through steps slowly over several days
- You may pause after any step and return later
- You may repeat a single step until it feels complete
- You never need emotional intensity to heal
- The body's timing is sacred

Shadow work is not about removing darkness.
It is about shining truth —
softly, steadily —
until every frightened part of you knows it is safe.

This layout is a doorway
to the inner home that waited years for your return.

Bibliography

Jung & Shadow Theory

- Jung, Carl G. *Aion: Researches into the Phenomenology of the Self.* Princeton University Press, 1978.
- Jung, Carl G. *The Archetypes and the Collective Unconscious.* Princeton University Press, 1981.
- Johnson, Robert A. *Owning Your Own Shadow: Understanding the Dark Side of the Psyche.* HarperOne, 1991.
- Zweig, Connie, and Steve Wolf. *Meeting the Shadow: The Hidden Power of the Dark Side of Human Nature.* Penguin Putnam, 1997.

Trauma, Nervous System, and Somatic Memory

- van der Kolk, Bessel. *The Body Keeps the Score: Brain, Mind, and Body in the Healing of Trauma.* Viking, 2014.
- Levine, Peter A. *Waking the Tiger: Healing Trauma.* North Atlantic Books, 1997.
- Ogden, Pat, Kekuni Minton, and Clare Pain. *Trauma and the Body: A Sensorimotor Approach to Psychotherapy.* W. W. Norton, 2006.
- Maté, Gabor. *In the Realm of Hungry Ghosts.* Vintage Canada, 2010.
- Siegel, Daniel J. *The Developing Mind: How Relationships and the Brain Interact to Shape Who We Are.* Guilford Press, 2012.

Inner Child, Attachment, and Emotional Imprinting

- Bradshaw, John. *Homecoming: Reclaiming and Championing Your Inner Child.* Bantam, 1990.
- Gibson, Lindsay C. *Adult Children of Emotionally Immature Parents.* New Harbinger Publications, 2015.
- Crittenden, Patricia M. *Raising Parents: Attachment, Parenting, and Child Safety.* Willan Publishing, 2008.
- Schore, Allan N. *Affect Regulation and the Origin of the Self.* Routledge, 2003.

Belief Systems, Self-Identity & Subconscious Work

- Dispenza, Joe. *Breaking the Habit of Being Yourself.* Hay House, 2012.
- Tolle, Eckhart. *The Power of Now.* New World Library, 1997.
- Schwartz, Richard C., and Martha Sweezy. *Internal Family Systems Therapy.* Guilford Press, 2019.

Energy Healing, Chakra Psychology & Aura-Based Perspectives

- Brennan, Barbara Ann. *Hands of Light: A Guide to Healing Through the Human Energy Field.* Bantam, 1987.
- Judith, Anodea. *Eastern Body, Western Mind: Psychology and the Chakra System as a Path to the Self.* Celestial Arts, 1996.
- Eden, Donna. *Energy Medicine.* TarcherPerigee, 1998.
- Leadbeater, Charles W. *The Chakras.* Quest Books, 1972.

Mind–Body Spirituality, Compassion, and Self–Reclamation

- Neff, Kristin. *Self-Compassion: The Proven Power of Being Kind to Yourself.* William Morrow, 2011.
- Frankl, Viktor E. *Man's Search for Meaning.* Beacon Press, 1959.
- Brown, Brené. *The Gifts of Imperfection.* Hazelden Publishing, 2010.
- Chödrön, Pema. *When Things Fall Apart: Heart Advice for Difficult Times.* Shambhala Publications, 1997.

Nervous System Regulation & Breathwork

- Rosenberg, Stephen W. *Accessing the Healing Power of the Vagus Nerve.* North Atlantic Books, 2017.
- Nestor, James. *Breath: The New Science of a Lost Art.* Riverhead Books, 2020.

Intergenerational Trauma & Subconscious Inheritance

- Schore, Allan N. *Right Brain Psychotherapy.* W. W. Norton, 2019.
- Bridgman, Thomas. *Inherited Trauma and the Science of Memory.* Academic Press, 2021.
- Wolynn, Mark. *It Didn't Start with You: How Inherited Family Trauma Shapes Who We Are and How to End the Cycle.* Penguin Random House, 2016.

Spiritual

- Myss, Caroline. *Anatomy of the Spirit.* Harmony Books, 1996.
- Aponte, Jorge L. *The Quantum Body: Healing Through Energy Awareness.* SoulPress, 2018. *(fits well with your Tesla influence)*

Message From The Author

There were times in my life when I thought silence was
strength —
that being quiet, composed, and "fine" meant I had healed.

It took years to understand that silence was not evidence of
peace.
It was evidence of how young I was when I first learned to
protect myself.

Like many, my shadow began forming long before I had
language for fear, confusion, intuition, or inner knowing. I
didn't understand what I sensed, absorbed, or carried — only
that I felt it. And for a long time, I interpreted that weight as
proof that something in me was broken.

It wasn't.

And neither are you.

The shadow is a mirror passed down through atmosphere,
family stories, unspoken emotional rules, and the invisible
electricity inside a home. It is the history of what you
survived — and the brilliance of how you adapted to what
you could not yet understand.

Writing this book has been a return to the places inside
myself that learned to stay quiet, watch closely, care too

deeply, and disappear when necessary. It has been a reclamation of the child who once believed that survival required shrinking.

If you are holding this book, perhaps you know that feeling too.

I did not write these pages to retell wounds, nor to stir old pain. I wrote them so that no one would ever have to walk their inner world alone, or mistake their survival patterns for flaws.

Your shadow is not the sign of something wrong with you. It is the echo of something you outgrew.

Every freeze response, every instinct to protect, every moment your voice hid in your throat — these were not failures. They were wisdom. They were strategies. They were the body's genius response to conditions that asked far too much of someone small.

And now, as you stand here as an adult, you have earned the right to meet those parts of yourself with compassion instead of judgment.

This work is not about forcing memory, digging for trauma, or reliving the past. It is about creating the inner safety needed for your body to soften, your voice to return, and your truth to breathe again.

It is about the gentle courage of sitting beside your younger self and saying:

"You did nothing wrong.
You survived.
And I'm here now."

There is no perfection required.
No timeline.
No finish line.

Healing is not proving you are strong.
It is remembering that you always were.

If your shadows have felt heavy…
I hope these pages help you see the gifts they carried.

If parts of you still feel small…
I hope you discover how profoundly wise they truly are.

And if you have ever felt alone in your story…
I hope you feel accompanied here.

Thank you for choosing to step into this inner conversation.
Thank you for being willing to see yourself more clearly.
Thank you for meeting your own history with tenderness.

May this book be a lantern —
not to chase away your shadows,
but to illuminate the truth they've been guarding all along.

With compassion,
and deep respect for your journey,
Dr. Constance Santego

About The Author

Dr. Constance Santego is a natural medicine doctor, Grand Reiki Master, bestselling author, educator, and founder dedicated to the principles of emotional, energetic, and spiritual healing. For more than two decades, she has taught students around the world how to reconnect with their innate intelligence, reclaim their inner power, and awaken the healer within.

Her life's work began from a deeply personal understanding of shadow and survival. As a young mother, she made the decision to redefine her story, seek truth, and pursue inner freedom — a journey that led her through counselling, self-discovery, dedicated study, and ultimately into the mastery of Reiki, energy medicine, mind-body healing, and holistic traditions.

Dr. Santego has written over seventy books on spiritual development, energy healing, bioenergetics, intuitive awakening, and transformative inner work. Her teachings have formed the foundation for courses, workshops, manuals, therapy systems, practitioner certifications, and healing models that continue to support people in more than twenty countries.

She has trained thousands of students in Reiki and energetic healing modalities, created methodologies rooted in coherent frequency, inner-child reconnection, and emotional release, and supported practitioners, seekers, and everyday individuals in learning to trust their intuition and embrace their own spiritual gifts.

As a teacher, her voice is grounded, compassionate, and deeply human. Guided by lived experience, professional practice, and a lifelong dedication to growth, her approach blends ancient wisdom with modern understanding of trauma, energy, consciousness, and the intelligence of the nervous system.

As an author, her mission is simple:

To help people remember who they are beneath the wounds — and return to themselves with compassion.

Today, she continues to write, teach, mentor, and develop healing frameworks that honour both shadow and light. Through her books, teachings, and presence, she hopes to remind every reader that the parts of themselves once hidden for safety are not their weakness — but their wisdom.

She lives in British Columbia, Canada, surrounded by the mountains, lakes, and landscapes that inspire many of her stories, and remains devoted to sharing knowledge, supporting healing practitioners, and guiding others toward inner wholeness.

ALSO AVAILABLE

Play the game *Ikona* – Discover Your Inner Genie

For additional information on

Constance Santego's

wide range of Motivational Products, Coaching Sessions,
Spiritual Retreats,
Live Events and Educational Programs

Go to

www.ConstanceSantego.ca

Follow on Instagram – Constance_Santego and
Facebook – constancesantegoo

Subscribe and receive Free Information and Meditations on
my
YouTube Channel – Constance Santego

www.ingramcontent.com/pod-product-compliance
Lightning Source LLC
Chambersburg PA
CBHW071707120626
46550CB00001B/135